BY BRIAN TIPPETTS

# Get Creative
# WITH TYPE

*Fun typography ideas and tips for scrapbooking*

# "HEY, BRIAN! What's that font in those ads that always looks really cool?"

**THAT'S AN EXAMPLE** of a common phrase hollered between my office and Brian's when I've found a cool new font on a website or print ad that I want to use on a scrapbook page (why bother with phones when there's a single wall that divides our work spaces?). I could spend hours typing "The quick brown fox jumped over the lazy dog" to find the right font for the look I'm after, or I could just ask our resident type pro, Brian.

That's the lazy approach, though. If I'm feeling a little more energetic, I'll walk right over to his office to show him the font in question, and without a doubt he'll identify it in two seconds flat. I remember showing him my Kate Spade wallet and asking him what font the logo was because I wanted to use it on a scrapbook page. "It looks like Baskerville" he said—I must say, I was quite satisfied with the results on my page!

The CK team has long relied on Brian as the one-stop source for design wisdom, but if you've never worked with him, a quick glance around his office is sufficient proof that the man knows (and loves) type. Artfully carved wooden letters perched atop his bulletin board demand attention, and a plump pillow adorned with swoopy t's, p's and q's invites you to sit down in the armchair adjacent to his desk (which, incidentally, is stacked with magazines and catalogs from cool design-y sources like Veer and Communication Arts).

Simply put, if anyone could present typography as a useful, inspiring scrapbooking tool, it would be Brian, and he's done just that in this amazing book. He and his talented team of scrapbookers will educate and inspire you with ideas for evoking memories, emotions and stories just by arranging words and letters in a fun, new way.

As Brian would say, "Enjoy!"

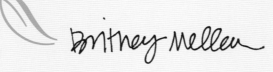

**PERFECT COZY MORNING** *by Britney Mellen*

HOW cool! Britney's page title was inspired by one of her favorite cookbooks and also uses Adobe's Serifa Bold font and similar letter colors as the book's title. Notice how she created her title block on a photo before printing it out and adding it to her page.

**SIMPLY ORGANIC** *by Jesse Ziff Cool, Chronicle Books*

# scrapbooking = DESIGN

**MY MANY YEARS** in the scrapbooking industry have brought me to one very big conclusion: Scrapbooking and design go hand in hand. As designers and scrapbookers, we use color, pattern, texture, repetition, focus, context, shape, proportion, photography and type to convey our message. Of all these factors, type (letters, words, titles and journaling) has always been a passion of mine. I love:

• How each letter and number has it own unique qualities and characteristics.

• Swashes, ligatures, initial caps and the many surprises that are found within fonts.

• Choosing just the right typeface to convey my message.

• How type design adds so much depth to the conversation.

• That even though I've seen thousands of typefaces, I still feel inspired by new fonts.

As scrapboookers, I know you're just as passionate about type as I am. You love:

• Downloading new fonts.

• Shopping for letter stickers, chipboard, rub-ons, stamps and more.

• Discovering creative ideas to alter your lettering products.

• Learning new tricks for making your computer-generated titles and journaling look cool.

• Creating beautiful pages where your photos and text work together to tell your stories.

Type is such an integral part of scrapbooking. As you read this book, I hope you'll get great ideas for fun title treatments and journaling solutions you can't wait to try on your own pages. And along the way, I hope you'll pick up some designer tricks for making your titles and journaling look sharper than ever. Watch for the tips I've added throughout this book that point out what's cool and why.

Ready for some fun with type? Jump in!

# Contents

# type profiles

### BRIAN TIPPETTS

**What's your favorite font?**

I have several favorite fonts. Right now, I'm in love with script fonts, like Feel Script from Veer, which has a variety of "extras" built in, like variations for characters at the beginning and ending of words, ligatures and more. I also like Cocktail Shaker, which is used in our *Creating Keepsakes* logo and cover. It has a spirit about it that makes me happy.

**What font are you?**

I feel like I'm Gotham but may vary within the family at times. Why? Gotham represents stability and consistency, and it's a workhorse.

### ALI EDWARDS

**What's your favorite font?**

Avenir. I use it all the time. It is clean + classic + sans serif, and I find myself turning to it over and over again. I tend to go through phases with favorite fonts, so I wouldn't be surprised if it changes again soon.

**What font are you?**

I would be Garamond or Baskerville. Both are classic and strong with those great serifs.

### AMANDA PROBST

**What's your favorite font?**

Sketch Rockwell. Rockwell itself has always been a favorite, so finding this cool version just makes me happy!

**What font are you?**

Century Gothic. Without a doubt. It's an incredibly practical and straight-forward font but with a wee bit of personality to make it distinct. It's versatile and secure in its own simplicity. It's reliable and constant and strikes me as nicely "organized."

### AMY MARTIN

**What's your favorite font?**

I've been partial to CK Classical for the last year or so. It's got just enough of a handwritten look without looking too messy.

**What font are you?**

I'm CK MixNMatch . . . a little bit clean, a little bit grungy with a dash of the unexpected, all working together seamlessly for the perfect combination.

### BRITNEY MELLEN

**What's your favorite font?**

CK Roxy. It's my go-to font when I want a project to have a hip, retro vibe.

**What font are you?**

CK Peaches. What could be more "me" than my own handwriting?

### DEENA WUEST

**What's your favorite font?**

It's a tie. Avant Garde is my go-to font for all the reasons listed below. Right beside it is Establo. I love that it's a bolder lowercase font with modern lines. Perfect for titles.

**What font are you?**

Avant Garde. It's clean, simple, modern . . . timeless. It's a solid foundation for any layout to which you can add accessory fonts like Garamond, Trashed, CK Ali and more.

### ELIZABETH KARTCHNER

**What's your favorite font?**

Mia's Scribblings. I love using it on pages about my little girls.

**What font are you?**

Decker. It's simple, easy-going and can easily be mixed with stylish and funky fonts.

### HEIDI SWAPP

**What's your favorite font?**

I love a good serif font. There are way too many for me to choose a favorite, but I really like Fashion Compressed.

**What font are you?**

Any font that's "all mixed up." Is there a font that mixes upper- and lowercase, script and serif . . . none of which lines up along the bottom? That would be me: completely disorganized and pulling it off!

### JENNIFER McGUIRE

**What's your favorite font?**

American Typewriter is my current favorite. It just seems to work for any style project, and it has a timeless feel.

**What font are you?**

VIP. It's a font that has basic letters for lowercase and fancy cursive letters for uppercase. That somewhat fits my style—sometimes simple and sometimes over the top.

### JESSICA SPRAGUE

**What's your favorite font?**

If you mean the one I use all the time, it's definitely Century Gothic. Clean, simple, readable and go-to.

**What font are you?**

Well, it's a toss-up between Century Gothic (on plainer days) and You Are Loved—a grunged-up, slightly off-kilter block sans serif that gives a soft, worn, comfy feel. Yep. That sounds just like me.

### KELLY PURKEY

**What's your favorite font?**

My current font obsession is Shag Mystery from House Industries.

**What font are you?**

I'm SP Purkage—a font I made from my handwriting. I also think I'm a little Metroscript: curvy, girly and stylish.

### LAURA KURZ

**What's your favorite font?**

Splendid 66 is definitely my default journaling font right now. I also love Fling for title work.

**What font are you?**

I'm something like Century Gothic—traditional with a little bit of funk and flair.

### MAGGIE HOLMES

**What's your favorite font?**

If I had to choose a favorite, I would say FranKlein, but in all actuality it depends on what I'm working on and the mood I'm trying to convey.

**What font are you?**

Modern No. 20—clean, friendly, stylish yet timeless. I like to be organized, and my style is very modern and clean yet warm and inviting with a bit of an eclectic twist.

### MOU SAHA

**What's your favorite font?**

Arial Narrow . . . yeah, I know, sounds boring! But, I've seen its great potential for fitting in tight spots while maintaining legibility. And if I'm not über-pressed for space, I like to play with Typo Upright BT.

**What font are you?**

I think I'm my own handwriting. Why? Because I like to be innovative and make something unique with a handmade touch.

### NICOLE LaRUE

**What's your favorite font?**

I don't think I could just pick one and say that it would stay the same forever. Right now, it would be Geometric 415. It's the one I use the most, though it's often paired with something a little more playful.

**What font are you?**

Something hand-drawn . . . by me! Something a bit more playful, unpredictable and a tad bit edgy. Why? Because that's what my life is about—it's playful and unpredictable; nothing is ever all too terribly straightforward, and that's what makes it so much fun!

DESIGN

# Section ONE

**ONE OF MY FAVORITE** classes in the graphics program at Brigham Young University was my Typography Design class. We studied the history and anatomy of type, and explored the many typestyles available at the time. I loved playing around with different fonts and choosing just the right typeface for each project I worked on. I discovered the importance of great type design and how it enhances a piece's overall look.

In scrapbooking, the same design principles apply—and choosing the right typestyle for your layout can improve its overall design. Join me as we examine some of the ways you can use type as an effective tool for design and communication.

# Communicating with TYPE

## chapter 1.1

How does type help with communication? Type is everywhere—it's how we convey information. We can't go through a day without communicating or being communicated to. We read newspapers, magazines, books, e-mails, websites and blogs. We see road signs; signs posted in stores and post offices and banks; packaging for groceries, electronics, hardware, appliances and so much more.

That's why as scrapbookers, we're passionate about fonts and lettering products (plus, they're just so much fun!). Read on for designer type tips!

"You cannot NOT communicate." —paul watzlawick

# how do i know what type to choose?

WITH SO MANY TYPE CHOICES AVAILABLE IN FONTS, STICKERS, CHIPBOARD AND MORE, CHOOSING THE RIGHT TYPEFACE CAN BE CHALLENGING. HERE ARE SOME TIPS:

① CONSIDER LEGIBILITY OR READABILITY. The reason for having type on your scrapbook page is to communicate, so make sure your readers can read what you've written!

- Is the typeface easy to read?

- Is the type the right size? Who's the audience for your page? Will he or she be able to read it without squinting?

- Is the type in a color that provides enough contrast against the background color? Will the type stand out against the background?

- Are there any distracting images or patterns behind the text? If you're printing on a photo, do you have a section of white space large enough to hold your text? If you're adhering stickers to patterned paper, is the print subtle enough that your title will be visible over it? What can you do to minimize distractions?

② DECIDE ON THE FOCUS OF YOUR PAGE. What do you want the main focus of the layout to be—the photo or the type? Usually, the focus of your page is going to be a photo. You can use type to create a visual hierarchy and support the focus of the page.

- Is the type distracting?

- Does the type pull my eye away from my focal-point photo?

- Does the type provide a nice complement to my photos?

③ THINK ABOUT THE APPROPRIATENESS OF THE TYPEFACE. Choose typefaces that will enhance your layout and support your page theme.

- Does the type match the personality of the scrapbook page? What's the look and feel? What's the mood?

- Is the type appropriate for the subject matter?

- Do I like the way it looks on my page?

# typeface classifications

HERE ARE SIX COMMON STYLES OF TYPE TO CONSIDER AS YOU CHOOSE TYPEFACES FOR YOUR PAGES:

- **Serif.** These letterforms have small lines finishing off the main strokes of a character. This is the most used style of type. Times New Roman, Palatino, Garamond, Caslon and Baskerville are examples of serif typefaces.

- **Sans Serif.** These letterforms don't have the small decorative finishing lines of serif fonts. These typefaces are generally used for headings and subheadings. Arial, Helvetica, Futura and Optima are examples of sans serif typefaces.

- **Script.** These typefaces are cursive letterforms that resemble handwriting. Letters in this style often connect. This style is used on ads, invitations, announcements and greeting cards. Brush Script, Edwardian Script, Fling, Memimas, MVB Café Mimi and Snell Roundhand are examples of script typefaces.

- **Display.** These typefaces are sometimes called decorative, novelty or occasional fonts. They're generally used for titles, advertising and headlines as they look best in larger sizes. Blackletter, Bodoni Poster, Impact, Gigi and Rosewood are examples of display typefaces.

- **Symbols.** These typefaces feature punctuation, dingbats, printer's ornaments and icons. They're generally used in conjunction with other type styles or for signage. Adobe Woodtype Ornaments, Dingbats, Webdings and Wingdings are examples of symbol typefaces.

- **Handwriting.** These typefaces have a more casual feel and are based on handwriting. They're used for titles, subtitles and short blocks of text. Comic Sans, Emma Script, Handsome, Mistral and Wendy are examples of handwriting typefaces.

# what makes a font readable?

THE EASIEST FONTS TO READ ARE SIMPLE SERIF FONTS
THAT ARE PROPERLY CAPITALIZED.

Most of the material we read (newspapers, books, magazines) is set in a serif font; because it's familiar, it's often the most comfortable type for us. Some designers suggest that serif fonts are more legible because they have "feet" that lead the eye from one letter to the next, making blocks of text easier to read.

When you're reading, your eye first identifies each letter at the x-height. Ascenders and descenders add additional detail, making it easier for your eye to differentiate between letterforms and word forms. Text set in all caps lacks ascenders and descenders—these missing identification marks make letterforms difficult to distinguish. Decorative fonts tend to be more visually complex and may include exaggerated details, making the text even more challenging to read.

## WHAT DOES THIS MEAN?

- For large blocks of journaling, choose a simple serif font.
- For smaller blocks of journaling, a serif or sans-serif font is fine.
- Sans-serif fonts look great as titles and subtitles.
- If you choose to use all caps on a title, make sure you use short words and set them in a sans-serif font.
- If you choose to use a complex, decorative font, use it on a title and capitalize only the first letter.

# anatomy of a typeface

THESE ARE THE FOUR MAIN PARTS OF A LETTER:

- **Baseline.** The imaginary line that a line of text rests on. Most typefaces have an even baseline, but some styles have letters that sit slightly above or below the baseline to create a distressed or spontaneous look.
- **X-height.** The lowercase character height when ascenders and descenders are excluded.
- **Ascender.** The lowercase letter stem that rises above the x-height, as in b, d or k. The height of the ascender is normally the same height as capital letters.
- **Descender.** The lowercase letter stem that falls below the baseline, as in p, g or y.

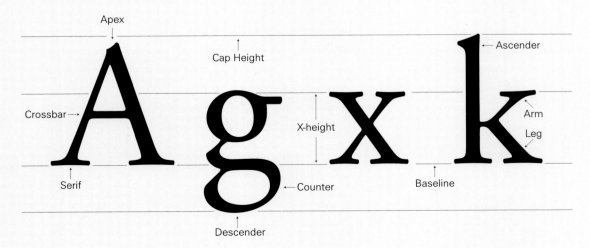

# do's and don'ts of typography

## DO:

① MAKE IT LEGIBLE. Choose typefaces that are easy to read.

② MAKE SURE YOUR TYPE SIZE IS LARGE ENOUGH TO READ. Journaling fonts should be 9–13 points. Decorative fonts should be at least 18 points. *Tip:* Remember that a 14-point sans-serif font is larger than a 14-point serif font.

③ CHOOSE A BOLD TYPEFACE if you're reversing out the font color to white.

④ PAY ATTENTION TO SPACING. Adjust line spacing (leading) to make journaling blocks easy to read and aesthetically appealing. Adjust the spaces between letters (kerning) on titles to prevent awkward gaps.

⑤ MAKE SURE ALL THE CHARACTERS YOU NEED ARE AVAILABLE IN THE FONT YOU CHOOSE. Some free fonts don't include punctuation or numbers.

## DON'T:

① USE ALL CAPS WHEN YOU USE A DECORATIVE FONT. It will be too visually complex and difficult to decipher.

② MIX MORE THAN THREE FONTS TOGETHER ON A SINGLE PROJECT—unless, of course, you're going for that ransom-note look. Remember that you can apply a color, a bold typeface or italics to words for emphasis without adding an additional font.

③ SPLICE YOUR JOURNALING BETWEEN A TWO-PAGE LAYOUT. It may look just fine when your layout is in progress on your work surface, but it will be hard to read in your album.

④ FORGET TO GO BACK AND TWEAK JUSTIFIED TEXT. Add or remove words or adjust column widths to fix spacing problems like gaps and a too-short last line.

⑤ BREAK UP TITLE WORDS INTO ODD CHUNKS. It confuses your visual message.

## DESIGNER'S EDGE: DETAILS TO MAKE YOUR TEXT LOOK SHARP!

① USE "SMART QUOTES" FOR QUOTATIONS (these are the "curly" quote marks). Save the foot and inch marks for measurements.

② SAY GOODBYE TO TWO SPACES BETWEEN SENTENCES. Yes, you had to hit the space key twice back in the days of typewriters and early word-processing, but thanks to current typographic technology, it's unnecessary and looks clunky.

③ MAKE NUMERALS MORE READABLE by using a typeface like Caslon that has old-style numbers with ascenders and descenders.

④ DON'T ADJUST THE LETTER SPACING OF CURSIVE OR SCRIPT FONTS—especially if the letters connect. While we're talking letter spacing . . . avoid adding extra spaces between lowercase letters.

⑤ TAKE CARE TO ADJUST YOUR COLUMN WIDTHS AND LINE BREAKS, or edit your text to prevent stray words at the end of paragraphs or very short lines at the beginning of a second column.

. . . . . . . . . . . . . . . . . . . . . . . . . . . . . . . . . . . . . . . . . . .

"We READ BEST what we read MOST." —zuzana licko

# DESIGN
## Solutions

*chapter 1.2*

I love to watch my children hand-letter a message or title on a piece of paper. Usually, the first letters are big with excessive spacing. As the words progress, the letters become more condensed and tightly spaced. Eventually they run out of room at one end and write the last few letters really small or on the next line.

Have you ever run out of space on a layout when creating your title or journaling, or seen pages with spacing issues? Perhaps you've seen titles broken up in odd chunks (for example, something like:

> Art
> is
> tic

Is it Artistic or Art is tic?).
The problem with this and other common type problems is that it often affects the readability of your text.

As you consider how type will be placed on a layout, preplan your text to make sure it fits well and is readable. Good type solutions, whether for a title or journaling, can support and enhance the overall beauty of your layout. On the following pages, take a look at how these designers have used type effectively.

"I chose Rockwell for the journaling because it's a FAVORITE OF MINE. I like that it's a nice, EASY-TO-READ serif font, and fairly simple. I generally choose a SERIF FONT for lengthier journaling because the 'feet' create a visual line, making it easier for the EYE TO FOLLOW the text." —*amanda probst*

# Patience trick

I don't know why, but when we stop at traffic lights, the boys have seemingly always believed they have the power to make the light change. Over the years, this has taken different forms…yelling at the light repeatedly, clapping, chanting, etc. Lately, though, Asher has decided upon a method that demands to be recorded. It's his "patience trick" and I love it. Asher, apparently, makes the light change by simply waiting until it does. Really. It's become such a part of his routine, the other boys acknowledge that it works (though they still prefer not to wait) and refer to it by name. "Asher use patience trick," Micah will inform you. Occasionally, this spills over to other areas of life, and I obviously encourage it. After all, who couldn't use a patience trick every now and then?

**PATIENCE TRICK** *by Amanda Probst*

HOW cool! Amanda originally planned to include her journaling directly on the photo but found that it was too difficult too read, even against the plain background. Her solution? She went for a more graphic design and cut the cardstock to fill the entire space around her photo. First, she formatted her journaling in Adobe InDesign, using ovals to roughly represent the head and shoulders in her photo, and used the Text Wrap feature to follow the shapes. After printing the text out on a test sheet of paper and making sure everything lined up where she wanted, she printed it onto cardstock and cut the desired shape.

"Type can be **HARD TO READ** on a project when the title is broken into segments or the journaling is written in a hard-to-read cursive font. To **PREVENT THESE PROBLEMS,** I created a horizontal title on a single line and made it large and colorful so it would stand out on the page. Additionally, I chose a **LARGE, CLEAR FONT** for **MY JOURNALING** to ensure readability." —*amy martin*

**FRESH AIR** *by Amy Martin*

"After TYPING OUT the title in green, I wanted to TAKE ADVANTAGE of the 'O's in the title, so I changed the first 'O' to red to match the photos and FURTHER the tomato theme of my page." —— *mou saha*

So,
**FINALLY**
**we are**

# TOMATO
growers

Ashis and I had been trying to grow tomatoes for a little while now.
We did have a pretty good crop a few seasons back and then again this year.
Well, by a good crop, I meant about 8-10 tomatoes smaller than grapes in size.
We never eat them. I put them in a bowl on the breakfast table
& admire them morning, noon & night till they start to shrivel or rot.
## I think we should throw a party
in honor of
our fresh grown vine ripe itty bitty
darling
tomatoes.

**TOMATO GROWERS** *by Mou Saha*

HOW cool! Mix typefaces from a single font family on your layout to keep the look unified while adding visual interest. On this page, Mou used Futura Lt BT, Futura Md BT and Futura XBlk BT. Notice how she used color and size to emphasize different letters, words and lines of text.

"The even look that justified text gives journaling goes well with the clean, STREAMLINED look of this page." —*Laura Kurz*

She doesn't **jump** on the bed anymore, but rather puts her two front paws up and waits for us to lift her up. She is **asleep** in her dog bed upstairs when we go to work in the morning and asleep on the **couch** when we get home at night. She **understands** the word walk, so we have to spell it out in front of her. She licks her lips when you ask her if she's **hungry**. She gets groomed at Beth's Pampered Paws. On **walks**, she pulls us toward Camden's gate. She acts like she is just tolerating Camden, but we all know they are really best **friends**. She still **believes** someday she will catch a bunny rabbit in our backyard. She is mystified at the fact that squirrels can **climb** trees. She has one trick, and it is sit. She **loves** peanut butter.

She is almost **eight** years old, and is starting to go gray. We **love** her.

C *by Laura Kurz*

HOW *cool*! Justified text looks great when done right. To create a page using justified text that doesn't contain any awkward space issues, consider:
- Adding or removing extra words to make the lines more even in length.
- Avoiding having a single word or two on the last line of the paragraph.
- Adjusting the size of the font or the text box to best accommodate the text.
- Watching out for spacing "holes."

"I love the size, color and font of these letter stickers! I **CHOSE THEM** to aid the **VISUAL HIERARCHY** of my page—so you should first notice the photo, then the title, then the journaling." —*elizabeth Kartchner*

**EVEN THOUGH** *by Elizabeth Kartchner*

HOW cool! Elizabeth created a different layer for each line of her journaling in Photoshop. This allowed her to easily angle the lines and move them closer together.

"Don't be afraid to GO BIG WITH your journaling and devote an entire page to it. When you have a lot of journaling like this, make sure your typeface is large enough for your text to be LEGIBLE." —— *maggie holmes*

**9 MONTHS** *by Maggie Holmes*

HOW *cool*! When you're working with a large amount of journaling, take a cue from newspapers and magazines and consider formatting it into columns to enhance readability.

does a good job of putting
hands down to balance herse

just started making this face
a lot where she has her bottom lip
tucked in - **we adore it!**

can **roll over** both ways,
although she doesn't do it mu

BEFORE >>

AFTER ⌄

weight - 18.5 pounds
(down 1 pound from last month)

height - 29.25 inches

can **sit up** now all by herself
& does a good job of putting her
hands down to balance herself

just started making this face
a lot where she has her bottom lip
tucked in - **we adore it!**

can **roll over** both ways,
although she doesn't do it much

loves to be held & **cuddled**

**loves her daddy** & wants his
attention when he is around

**babbles** a lot more now -
says "mammama" & "babababa"

still loves her **bottles**

loves baby food - eats **3 jars** at a time

puts **everything** in her mouth

loves her **binkie,** especially
for naps & bedtime

loves the bath & started
**splashing** in it a few weeks ago

can go from **sitting** to her **tummy**

**laughs & giggles** at
Matthew in the car - he acts silly to her
& he calls her his "ga-ga"

loves all of her **blankies** – she pulls
them right up to her face when she is
tired & wants to go to sleep

is a **happy & sweet baby**
almost always - unless she is
hungry, tired or teething

likes to **play** pat-a-cake
& peek-a-boo

**sleeps** through the night -
from 8pm to about 7am

likes to play with **non-toys**
much more than regular toys - remote,
phone, keys, paper, etc

loves her **mama** & doesn't want
anyone else to hold her when
I am around (except for daddy)

has 4 **teeth** now with 3 more
on the way - 3 on the bottom, one on top
& 3 on top coming in

**& my favorite thing**
that she just started doing - when I am
holding her on my hip she will lay her
head down on my shoulder –
it absolutely **melts my heart!!**

who emily jane
what 9 month stats
where gilbert, AZ
when April 11, 2008

LEADING tip! If you change the size or weight of key words within a document, make sure
you change the leading of the text to avoid irregular line spacing. To do this in Microsoft
Word, click the "Format" button on your toolbar, then select "Paragraph." Under the line spacing dropdown menu, choose "Exactly" and set a point size that is large enough to comfortably
accommodate the largest letters in your text.

# Color + TYPE

## chapter 1.3

Using colored type can add visual impact to your layout as well as create an emotional connection. When I designed the covers for *Creating Keepsakes* magazine, I played with color and type to make the call-outs jump out to the reader. I'd often experiment with colors I hadn't used before and had fun placing the type over backgrounds to see how the colors interacted with each other.

Color makes a huge impact on everything—including type! Adding color to type or choosing colorful lettering products can add vibrancy to a layout. Use it to:
• Energize your text.
• Emphasize letters, words or phrases.
• Attract your reader's attention.
• Complement your page design.

As you choose colors for your type, remember that color creates additional visual complexity on your page and impacts several facets of your layout, including the:
• Legibility of your title or journaling.
• Focus and visual hierarchy of the page.
• Mood or emotion of the page.

"For the title, I mimicked one of the graphic designs from the photos to create a frame for the FOCAL-POINT photo and a home for the title. I chose these title letters because they fit, were easy to paint and CONTRASTED nicely with the JOURNALING font. I also liked that they're very round, similar to the target itself." —*amanda probst*

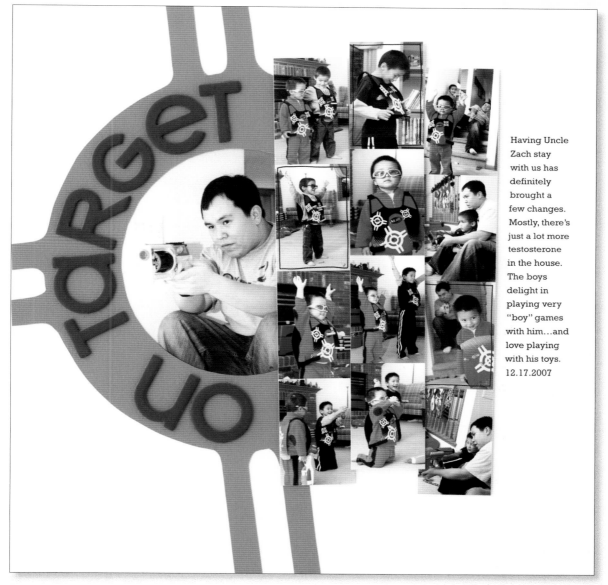

Having Uncle Zach stay with us has definitely brought a few changes. Mostly, there's just a lot more testosterone in the house. The boys delight in playing very "boy" games with him...and love playing with his toys. 12.17.2007

**ON TARGET** *by Amanda Probst*

HOW cool! The blue letters on the orange background give Amanda a dramatic page title. When working with colored type on a colored background, make sure there's enough contrast between the colors to ensure your text is easy to read.

"I like the straight-forwardness of this font. PAIRING IT with SEVERAL COLORS of ink really makes various words pop from the page." —Laura Kurz

**OURS** *by Laura Kurz*

HOW cool! Some colors will emphasize your text while others will make it recede into the background or fade out. Use color to direct the focus of your layout.

"I originally created this layout using soft peach and sage colors. The finished layout didn't CONVEY THE EMOTION I was looking for, so I punched it up with bold yellow and orange colors. The result? A BOLD LAYOUT that reflects my daughter's strong reaction to her first bite of peaches." —Deena Wuest

further
PROOF

that subtlety is not a natural trait

So tell me how you really feel. Shuddering...wincing...gagging... cringing...spitting? Your first taste of peaches wasn't as much an experience as it was a form of torture. Note to self: Buy PEARS!

Feb. 2008 : 5 months old

**FURTHER PROOF** *by Deena Wuest*

HOW cool! When you're choosing color for the type on your page, consider the emotion and symbolism the color represents. Think about how different this page would look and feel in the soft peach and sage green Deena originally intended to use, or how it might look in shades of blue or gray. The bright orange and yellow deliver a bold feeling of surprise appropriate for the page theme and photos.

"I chose this font and these stickers for the **YOUNG, PLAYFUL** feel they express. Using yellow, red and brown stickers, I spelled out some of the things **MY SON SAYS**. I typed out my 'translations' of his sayings using the Tigger font in black." ——mou saha 3

**AT 3** *by Mou Saha*

HOW cool! Notice how the black text below the colorful stickers acts as subtext and supports the bright, bold words and phrases.

GROW LIKE A WEED *by Amy Martin*

HOW cool! Reverse out the text on your digital pages to get the look of white text. When reversing out text, make sure the background is dark enough to make the white text pop.

"I chose Establo for the background text layer because it's a clean, CHUNKY FONT that can be easily read with type over it. For the journaling, I chose Shag Expert because it's a fun font that matches the feel of the words and is THIN ENOUGH to show the text behind it. I highlighted key words in the journaling for emphasis—mostly DESCRIPTIONS of Chloe." —*Kelly Purkey*

I am lucky to have a friend like Chloe. She has a witty and sarcastic humor that I love. She is an amazing listener who also tells great stories. She is always looking for adventure and entertainment in life. Like every nice girl that I know, she is very humble about how great a person she is. But I know that she is wonderful and we are all lucky to know her. So even if she doesn't see it herself, I don't mind having to remind her once in a while.

CHLOE

**CHLOE** *by Kelly Purkey*

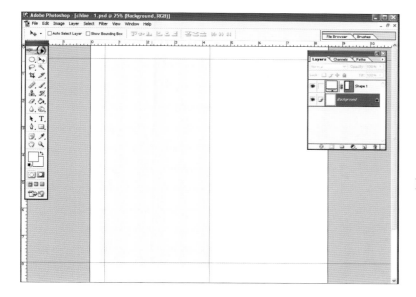

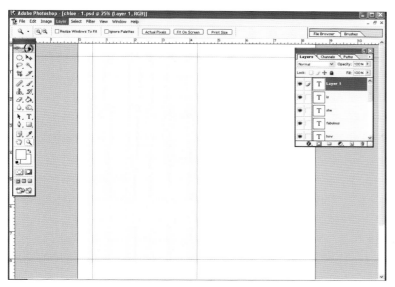

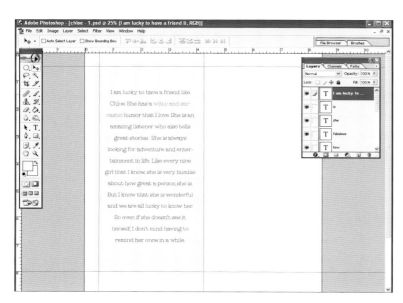

HOW cool! When layering two text blocks, choose lighter colors for the background text and reduce the opacity in order to keep the focus on the front text block. Want to create your own layered text block? Here's how you can get this look digitally using Photoshop Elements:

① OPEN a new letter document and drag guides onto the background. Add a solid-color rectangle.

② ADD text layers in different sizes. Use a color that is lighter than your background and bring the opacity of each text layer down to 75%.

③ ADD a text box with your journaling as your very top layer. Align and size it to be centered over the background text.

④ HIGHLIGHT important words of the journaling using a variety of colors from the color picker.

VARIATION: Get this look using traditional scrapbooking supplies, too! Stamp your background text using light ink or paint. Let it dry, then write your journaling over it using darker pens.

# PUNCTUATION &³ Dingbats

*chapter 1.4*

I love adding punctuation and dingbats to my design projects and layouts. Whenever I purchase or download a new font, I go through each keystroke to discover the hidden gems for that specific font. Often, I find a collection of dingbats that follow the look and feel of the typeface and provide a fantastic unifying effect when used with the font.

Use dingbats and punctuation:

- To add accents to your text.
- As stylish bullet points for lists.
- To separate sentences.
- To emphasize key words or phrases.
- To visually communicate an idea.

Some dingbats have a cool iconic nature that can quickly convey information to the reader. Think about the dingbats you see on road signs and what they mean. For example, a walking figure indicates a pedestrian crossing, an arrow points us in a certain direction, and a tent signifies a camping area.

For a class assignment in college, I had to create a set of information icons that could be understood at a glance. It was fun to research, then sketch and simplify each icon to be a "quick read." Look at some commonly used themes in your layouts and create a set of icons to use on your pages. Or, search your favorite font websites for cool downloadable dingbats that are ready to go!

"I picked this TYPEFACE because of the storybook-style INITIAL CAPS that were part of the font family. Notice the cute crown dingbats—they're INCLUDED in the Gigi font." —— *brian tippetts*

ONCE UPON A TIME... THERE LIVED THREE PRINCESSES ♛ THEY LOVED TO TRAVEL THE WORLD IN SEARCH OF OTHER PRINCESSES ♛ ONE DAY THEY CAME UPON A MAGICAL PRINCESS NAMED JASMINE ♛ AND THEY LIVED HAPPILY EVER AFTER ♛ *Disneyland 2007*

**ONCE UPON A TIME** *by Brian Tippetts*

HOW cool! Use dingbats within your journaling to separate sentences or paragraphs.

"This was a fun page to put together, mainly because of the many different LETTERING TYPES: chipboard, fonts and my handwriting."

—brian tippetts

AMY *by Brian Tippetts*

HOW cool! If your chipboard alphabet doesn't include parenthesis symbols, just cut a capital "O" down the middle lengthwise.

"Here, I used FONTS AND COLOR to help the reader distinguish between my son's voice and my voice. Using one font for his words and another for mine makes it EASY TO FOLLOW the conversation." —*deena wuest*

**a daily conversation**

I love you. You're my BEST mom!
aww, thanks! you're my best baby!
Mommmm! I'm not a baby!
oh, I'm sorry! you're my best boy!
Nooo! Mom! I'm not a boy!
then what are you?
You know. I'm your Skyler Wuest!
then you're my best skyler wuest!
Thanks! You're my best mom!

skyler wuest best my !

(almost four)

**MY BEST SKYLER WUEST** *by Deena Wuest*

HOW cool! Use punctuation marks as icons or accents. Here, Deena used a large exclamation point to hold her page title. To do this, she enlarged an exclamation point to fill the space, then typed in each word of her title. She enlarged and rotated the text until it fit nicely inside the exclamation point. Then she clipped each text layer to the shape layer by hitting Ctrl+G to ensure that the edges of each letter were contained neatly inside the shape.

"For this layout, I printed out some CUTE CIRCLE DINGBATS and used the Dropper tool in Photoshop to change them from black to red and light turquoise to MATCH THE LAYOUT. I highlighted letters of the alphabet to create my page title and to share how this is Avery's favorite word to say at the MOMENT." —elizabeth Kartchner

NO *by Elizabeth Kartchner*

HOW cool! Get creative with dingbats, icons and punctuation marks! Try resizing and recoloring them, then print them directly on your page. Or, print them on cardstock or a transparency and cut them out before adhering them to your layout. You can also try inking the edges and applying Diamond Glaze for shine and dimension, or glitter for a fun, sparkly look.

"The circles **BEHIND THE TITLE** are dingbats called Cafeina Dig that I printed on a transparency. I used them to add spunk to my title and to **CREATE A HOME** for each of the letter stickers. I used two brackets in different styles to emphasize my title and **ADD VARIETY.**" —*maggie holmes*

**ROLLING** *by Maggie Holmes*

HOW cool! Dingbats, also called ornaments, are available in a wide variety of styles and themes from many of your favorite font sites. Use them to support the theme of your page or to emphasize certain page elements, as Maggie did here with her page title.

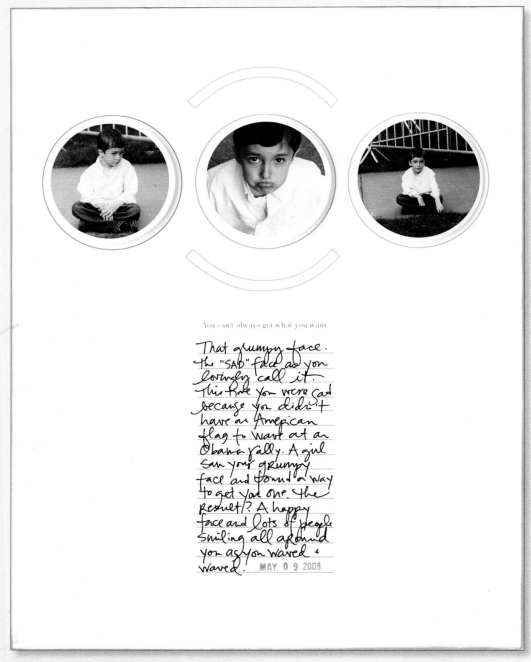

You can't always get what you want

*That grumpy face. The "SAD" face as you lovingly call it. This time you were sad because you didn't have an American flag to wave at an Obama rally. A girl saw your grumpy face and found a way to get you one. The result? A happy face and lots of people smiling all around you as you waved & waved.*

MAY 0 9 2008

**YOU CAN'T ALWAYS GET WHAT YOU WANT** *by Ali Edwards*

HOW cool! This sharp-looking page is easy to create! Just print circles, lines and accent type onto cardstock. Adhere photos and handwrite journaling onto the printed cardstock. Ink the edges and you're done!

# ali edwards on dingbats, icons and punctuation

**WE SAT DOWN WITH ALI EDWARDS TO TALK ABOUT USING DINGBATS, ICONS AND DECORATIVE PUNCTUATION ON SCRAPBOOK PAGES.**

**DINGBATS AND DECORATIVE PUNCTUATION ARE FUN TO USE, BUT WHEN AND WHY DO YOU USE THEM?**

I like to use them specifically to create homes for photos or other embellishments. They can work on any sort of page—the ones I choose to use are more generic, which gives me more flexibility in the overall design. I think it would be cool to use a single icon or punctuation mark as the basis for an entire mini book—print an enlarged dingbat onto cardstock, punch holes for rings and add content.

**WHAT'S COOL ABOUT DINGBATS?**

① They're graphic and most of them have very clean lines. I love graphic!

② They're free and easy to grab off the computer.

③ They can become homes for additional page elements or photos.

**WHAT TYPES OF ICONS DO YOU LIKE TO USE ON YOUR PAGES? WHY?**

① **Brackets.** I like putting content in between two of them—it's the whole concept of creating a home for other elements.

② **Circles.** Anything with circles! Circles are a go-to for me because they're simple and can easily be mixed with other circle embellishments.

③ **Life icons.** Telephones, computers, etc.—I love anything that can be used as an embellishment for documenting our everyday lives.

**WHAT ARE YOUR FAVORITE WAYS TO CUSTOMIZE OR EMBELLISH PUNCTUATION, DINGBATS OR ICON ACCENTS?**

① Color them on the computer before printing them out—they don't have to be black.

② Use just the outlines of the icon or punctuation mark. That's what I did on this layout.

③ Cut them out to create stencils.

**HOW DO YOU INCORPORATE DINGBATS AND ICONS INTO YOUR OVERALL DESIGN SCHEME?**

I like to place them on my pages first. Often I'll design the entire page around the dingbats, creating the foundation of the layout on my computer first. I'll then print out the page and add the photos and embellishments.

# Design FUN

*chapter 1.5*

The first class I taught at Creating Keepsakes University was called "What Is Your Personality Type?" In the class, I showed three versions of a scrapbook layout—each with a different typeface. Although the typeface was the only thing different on each version of the layout, students were amazed to see how it changed the look and feel of the entire page.

If you're looking for ways to try out a new style on a layout or thinking about doing a page makeover, changing up the typeface is an easy place to start. When you're choosing a new typeface, consider the following:
• Does it suit the mood of my page?
• Is it appropriate for my page's theme?
• Is it easy to read?

That said, don't be afraid to experiment with different typefaces. If you're using fonts, it's so easy to change up the look—be sure to try out a few new styles before making a decision.

## TYPE MAKEOVER

Even though a typeface may be very cute, sometimes it's just not a good choice for the layout you're working on. Take a look at these two pages to see how a type makeover enhances the overall look of the layout.

### BEFORE >>

This all-caps title features a thin, handwritten-style script font. While the whimsical nature of the font initially seems like a fun complement to the bright patterned papers and cute page accents, the title doesn't seem substantial enough to support the bold colors and patterns. Also, the script nature of the font makes an all-caps style difficult to decipher.

"This TITLE simply looks out of place and doesn't fit the page."

—amy martin

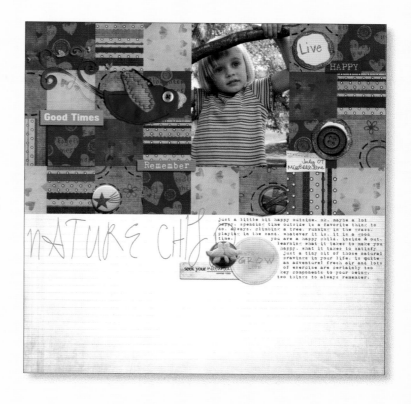

### << AFTER

This all-caps title features a distressed serif font. The distressing resembles a weather-worn stamped lettering style that reinforces the hand-crafted look of the fabric bird and the stitches in the patterned paper. The size and weight of the type is substantial enough to carry the bold design and patterns on the page.

"The THEME of this layout is nature, so a stamped TITLE FLOWS WELL with the rest of the design."

—amy martin

**NATURE CHILD** *by Amy Martin*

## CHOOSE THE BEST TYPE

We asked Amanda to create three versions of a page—each one featuring different font choices for her title and journaling. Take a look at all three pages, then decide which type treatment you like best.

## VERSION 1 ⌄

This title font has more personality than the other two options but is still easy to read and fits the style of the page. The sketchy aspect of the font and the handwriting style of the journaling complement the young subjects of the layout.

**A HELPING HAND** *by Amanda Probst*

HOW cool! Use these simple techniques to take various type-faces for a test run:

- **FONTS.** Type out your text and apply different typefaces to it.

- **LETTER STAMPS.** Stamp your text on a transparency and position it over your layout to see if it's the look you want. Use it as a guide as you stamp directly on your page.

- **LETTER STICKERS AND RUB-ONS.** Cut them out while they're still on the contact sheet and arrange them on your page. Apply them to your page after you get the look you want.

- **HANDWRITING.** Use a pencil first. When you're happy with the text, trace over it with a pen or marker. Allow the ink to dry, then erase the pencil marks.

""The **FIRST VERSION**—my favorite—features a simple but slightly fun and different title font. I **WANTED** it to be interesting but not distracting, as the **MAIN FOCUS** here is the photo sequence. Because the title is a **SERIF FONT**, I chose a sans-serif journaling font so the two wouldn't **COMPETE**."

—*amanda probst*

**VERSION 2** ⌃

These fonts are fine but don't express the theme and feel of the page as well as the first set of fonts.

"My SECOND-CHOICE version features typewriter fonts. I was GOING FOR a 'reporting the story' sort of feel and LIKED THE MORE youthful appearance of the OUTLINE TITLE font. The typewriter font for the journaling didn't LOOK RIGHT with a jagged edge, so I created a TEXT BOX using the full-justify feature."
—amanda probst

**VERSION 3** ⌃

This set of fonts provides more visual interest and contrast than the second set, but the fonts lack the youthful energy of the first set.

"The THIRD-CHOICE version is probably most typical of me, which MAY BE WHY I like the others better. I just wanted something PLAIN and SIMPLE and very straightforward. Using the font Impact as a title ALWAYS DOES that for me, as does using Rockwell as a journaling font."
—amanda probst

## MIX & MATCH TYPE

Can one typeface provide a variety of looks? You bet it can! We asked Deena and Kelly to match a single typeface with different type sizes, leading, kerning and colors. Take a look at the results!

"Using ONE FONT on a page or card creates a wonderfully cohesive look that's easy on the eyes. You can ADD INTEREST to your project by adjusting the size, color and spacing, like I did here."

—Deena Wuest

**"HAPPY BIRTHDAY" CARD** *by Deena Wuest*

HOW cool! Notice how Deena has plenty of visual interest in her text even though she only used one typeface. Her use of font color, background color, size, spacing and all-caps versus a mix of caps and lowercase letters lends a fun, playful look to this card.

"I chose Pretty Baby because it's a fun, EASY-TO-READ, girly font. I MIXED UP the sizes of the type and the leading to make the 'wishes' stand out as ONE THOUGHT in the jumble of text. This is kind of how my mind works, thinking of crazy ideas in BRIGHT little pieces." —*kelly purkey*

**ONE WISH** *by Kelly Purkey*

HOW cool! Did you have to do a double take to see if this was really just one typeface? Kelly's use of font size, color and leading makes her page compelling to view, while the single typeface gives it a unified feel.

# STYLE

# Section TWO

**ONE OF MY DESIGN PROFESSORS** once said, "There's only one typeface I don't want you to use . . . ." That typeface became my new best friend. I took on the challenge to use it in a way that would make it shine. I tried and tried . . . and to this day, I still haven't accomplished the feat of making it showcase-worthy. My point is that some typefaces just don't look right, regardless of how you try to use them. Plus, it's easy to get into a "font rut." When that happens, it's time to expand your horizons—and your font library. Be flexible and try several type options when you begin your design process.

When choosing typefaces, keep in mind that some styles will look dated in a few years—and that's okay. It's one more time marker to indicate where you are right now. Some of today's most popular typefaces include typewriter, handwritten and blackletter styles. Did you know that back in the fifteenth century, the blackletter style of type was considered the most popular and easiest to read? It was used for the original printing of the Gutenberg Bible. Today, it's considered youthful, edgy and borderline unreadable.

# top
# TYPEFACES
# for Themes

*chapter 2.1*

Choosing the right typeface for themed pages can be tricky. Why? Because type can evoke time periods, places, moods, emotions and events. Some fonts are automatically connected with specific themes. For example, if you're looking for a typeface to go with a western-themed party, fonts like Rosewood or Blackoak come to mind.

To make it a little easier for you to choose fonts for your next themed page or project, we've listed some of our favorites and some ideas to consider. Take a look then add a new font or two to your next page!

"YOU ROCK!" CARD *by Amanda Probst*

"When I think of fonts for BIRTHDAY cards, I think of happy, fun fonts." —*amanda probst*

## AMANDA'S TOP 5 FONTS
### FOR BIRTHDAY-THEMED PAGES

- CK Evie, *www.creatingkeepsakes.com*
- Kravitz, *www.scrapvillage.com*
- Pointy, *www.dafont.com*
- TXT Soda Shoppe, *www.scrapnfonts.com*
- Yippy Skippy, *www.fonts101.com*

Want a cute birthday-themed dingbat? Check out:
- DB Party Sketch, *www.scrapnfonts.com*

HOW cool! Amanda built a "birthday cake" using words as "cake" layers. To line them up just right, she put each word in its own text box. She printed her card in color, highlighted words with Glossy Accents from Ranger Industries and added extra color with Sakura's Glaze and Soufflé pens.

"I chose the Cairo font for the message because it's BOLD AND STANDS OUT against the large star design. I chose a dingbat called Seeing Stars to create the LARGE STAR on the front of the card. I love this dingbat because it has several different star designs you can print to create your own paper or use as ACCENTS ON CARDS or layouts." ——maggie holmes

**"HAPPY BIRTHDAY" CARD** *by Maggie Holmes*

## MAGGIE'S TOP 5 FONTS
### FOR BIRTHDAY-THEMED PAGES

- Big Mummy
- Bloc
- Cairo
- Suede
- UBahn

All fonts available for download at *www.dafont.com*.

"I love this **COOL BIRTHDAY-BANNER** font! It looks just like the banner we hang at our house for birthdays. I used it for the title, then duplicated it, **ENLARGED IT** and made it into an overlay for my background paper. I paired it with a fun and **CASUAL** font called Friends." —*deena Wuest*

**BIRTHDAYS** *by Deena Wuest*

HOW cool! Deena typed the words on her photo in separate text boxes, then tilted and positioned them so they look like they're emerging from the candle flames.

## DEENA'S TOP 5 FONTS
### FOR BIRTHDAY-THEMED PAGES

- CK Stenography, *www.creatingkeepsakes.com*
- Friends, *www.typenow.net/themed*
- JLR Birthday Banner, *www.fontspace.com*
- LB Hodge Podge, *www.creatingkeepsakes.com*
- Vaguely Repulsive, *www.abstractfonts.com*

## WEDDING

- Consider elegant script and formal serif typefaces for wedding pages.
- Look for typefaces with swashes, ligatures and coordinating dingbats that can be used to add lovely finishing touches to your text.
- *Remember:* Decorative typefaces may be more difficult to read. Make sure you size the font large enough to enhance readability.

## LAURA'S TOP 5 FONTS
### FOR WEDDING-THEMED PAGES

- Copperplate Gothic Light
- Georgia
- English
- Porcelain
- Scriptina

Copperplate Gothic Light and Georgia are from Microsoft. All other fonts are available for download at *www.dafont.com.*

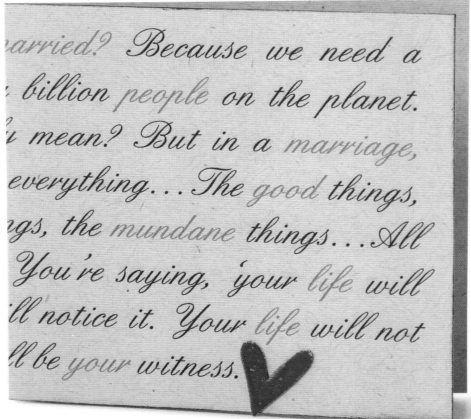

**YOUR WITNESS** *by Laura Kurz*

"I love using **SCRIPT FONTS** for wedding cards and layouts, and English is one of my favorites. It's elegant but still very **EASY TO READ.**" —*Laura Kurz*

"I like the elegance of Hancock and that it's **STILL A BOLD**, easy-to-read font. I **PAIRED IT** with Fling—a great font that's very stylish and trendy right now." —*Kelly Purkey*

**FATHER OF THE BRIDE** *by Kelly Purkey*

HOW *cool*! To create the butterfly accents, Kelly typed "Love" several times and printed the text on cardstock. She cut out butterflies from the printed cardstock and patterned paper using shape templates. To finish, she adhered the pieces together and used foam adhesive dots to pop up the hearts in the middle, giving the wings dimension.

## KELLY'S TOP 5 FONTS
### FOR WEDDING-THEMED PAGES

• Bickham Script
• Filosofia
• Fling
• Hancock
• Mrs. Eaves

Hancock is available for download at *www.simplythebest.net/fonts/*. All other fonts are available at *www.myfonts.com*.

## BABY

- Consider rounded-serif and sans-serif fonts for an open, youthful feel. Choose light weights for a soft look.

- Simple script or handwritten styles also look great on baby-themed pages.

## ELIZABETH'S TOP 5 FONTS
### FOR BABY-THEMED PAGES

- 2Peas Peanut Butter, *www.twopeasinabucket.com*
- 2Peas Sailboat, *www.twopeasinabucket.com*
- 2Peas Tubby, *www.twopeasinabucket.com*
- CK Love Note, *www.creatingkeepsakes.com*
- Little Days, *www.dafont.com*

"BABY QUINCY" CARD *by Elizabeth Kartchner*

HOW cool! Type the alphabet several times, then print it out on a piece of colored cardstock and use it as patterned paper. You can also get this look by using a stamp, as Elizabeth did here.

"The two fonts I used on this page are INSPIRATION AND PHARMACY. They're both curvy and sweet, just like the subject of the layout." —amy martin

A wee bit of heaven
Drifted down from above
A handful of happiness,
A heartful of love.
The mystery of life,
So sacred and sweet
The giver of joy
So deep and complete.
Precious and priceless,
So lovable, too
World's sweetest miracle,
Baby is you!
Helen Steiner Rice

A BORROWED BIT OF HEAVEN

Baby Boy

William
Charlies
4 months
Richmond
Virginia

**BABY BOY** *by Amy Martin*

HOW cool! Notice how Amy used digital brushes around her photos that complement the style of her title font.

## AMY'S TOP 5 FONTS
### FOR BABY-THEMED PAGES

- CK Elsie, *www.creatingkeepsakes.com*
- Inspiration ROB, *www.myfonts.com*
- LDJ Silly Sister, *www.scrapnfonts.com*
- MA Sexy, *www.dafont.com*
- Pharmacy, *www.dafont.com*

## HOLIDAY

- So many types of fonts look great on holiday pages! Give extra consideration to formal, retro, vintage or classic typefaces.

- Look for holiday dingbats to add a little extra flair to your text.

## MAGGIE'S TOP 5 FONTS
### FOR HOLIDAY-THEMED PAGES

- Fabianestem
- Freebooter
- Modern No. 20
- Reznor Broken
- Scrypticali

Modern No. 20 is available at *www.myfonts.com*. All other fonts are available at *www.dafont.com*.

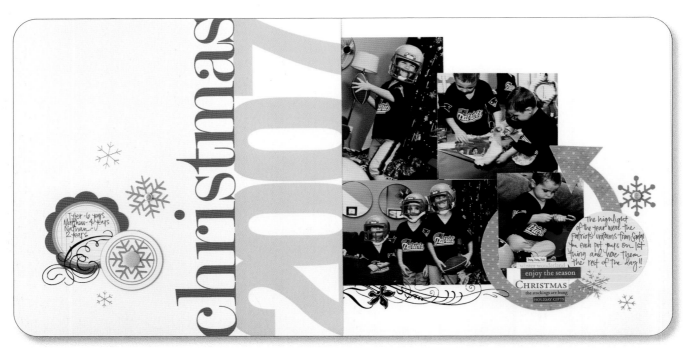

**CHRISTMAS 2007** *by Maggie Holmes*

"I love the **CLASSIC LOOK** of Modern No. 20. I think it fits perfectly with the holiday theme. I wanted the '2007' to be **BIG AND BOLD** and a little funky to contrast with the other font, so I chose Fabianestem. To personalize the page, I used **MY HANDWRITING** for my journaling." —*maggie holmes*

"**I CHOSE THESE FONTS** because the lightly distressed look works well with the Thanksgiving theme." —*elizabeth Kartchner*

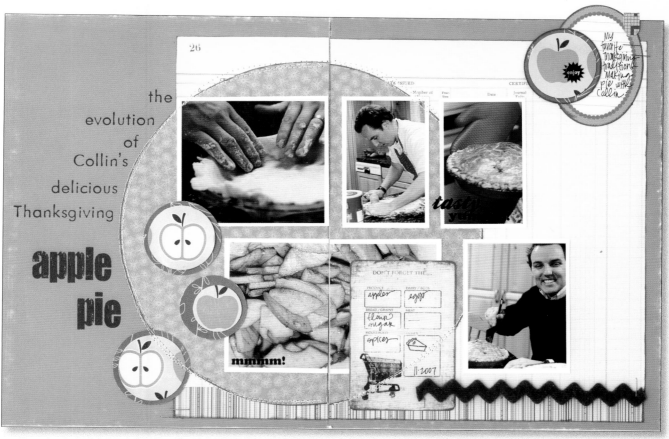

**APPLE PIE** *by Elizabeth Kartchner*

HOW cool! Try Elizabeth's title technique! In Photoshop, use the Shape tool to make a circle, then add your title around it. Delete the circle shape and print out your page. Cut out a patterned-paper circle in the same size as the one you created in Photoshop and adhere it in place.

## ELIZABETH'S TOP 5 FONTS
### FOR HOLIDAY-THEMED PAGES

- Valentine's Day: 2Peas Paisley
- Easter: 2Peas Easter
- Halloween: AL Scratched
- Thanksgiving: You Are Loved
- Christmas: 2Peas Bit O Honey

You Are Loved is available for download at *www.dafont.com*. All others are available at *www.twopeasinabucket.com*.

## TRAVEL

- Fonts and dingbats inspired by road signs add a fun element to travel pages.

- Did you know that it was easy to tell where you were in pre–World War II Europe just based on the typeface used on signage? If you travel internationally, consider vintage typefaces reminiscent of the countries you visit.

## LAURA'S TOP 5 FONTS
### FOR TRAVEL-THEMED PAGES

- Brandegoris
- Roman Grid Caps
- Splendid 66
- The Maple Origins
- Times New Yorker

All fonts available for download at *www.dafont.com.*

**KILLARNEY** *by Laura Kurz*

"I remember SEEING FONTS like Brandegoris when we visited Ireland, so when I saw this font, it immediately REMINDED ME of our trip. I PAIRED IT with the more traditional Times New Roman to get the title effect I was looking for." —*Laura Kurz*

"For this page, I chose fonts that REMIND ME OF SIGNAGE we saw on our travels. Tahoma and Impact are very basic and remind me of simple STREET SIGNS. Typist reminds me of the print on ticket stubs and boarding passes. I also ADDED ICONS for graphic appeal that's similar to the picture signs in airports." —*amanda probst*

**TRAVELOG** *by Amanda Probst*

HOW *cool*! Notice how Amanda used both a font and letter stickers to create her page title. Mixing the two letter types creates an effective distinction between the overlapping words.

## AMANDA'S TOP 5 FONTS
### FOR TRAVEL-THEMED PAGES

• CK Chemistry, *www.creatingkeepsakes.com*
• CK Surfer, *www.creatingkeepsakes.com*
• Impact, Microsoft
• Tahoma, Microsoft
• Typist, *www.searchfreefonts.com*

Want some cool travel icons? Check out the Webdings and Wingdings dingbats that come with your Microsoft software.

## HERITAGE

- Let the era of your photos direct your font choices. Look at memorabilia and old photos or search online for old movie posters, newspapers and advertisements.

- Vintage typewriter-inspired serif fonts and handwriting-inspired script fonts are also good choices.

## MOU'S TOP 5 FONTS
### FOR HERITAGE-THEMED PAGES

- American Typewriter, *www.fonts.com*
- Black Family, *www.dafont.com*
- Galleria, *www.fontstock.net*
- Typo Upright BT, *www.myfonts.com*
- Ribbonface, *www.vintagetype.com*

**AN ACTOR PREPARES** *by Mou Saha*

HOW cool! Notice how Mou used a hint of red and a single shaped word to make her title stand out.

"For this page, I chose Vintage Typewriter to get the VINTAGE look without SACRIFICING EASY READABILITY. I chose Galleria for style and drama, and American Typewriter for a little extra flair."

—mou saha

"I chose this **TITLE FONT** because I like its heritage feel, but it's still bold and stands out. I chose the **JOURNALING FONT** because it's classic and easy to read, yet doesn't seem too modern." —*maggie holmes*

**GRANDMA HANCEY** *by Maggie Holmes*

HOW *cool*! Maggie printed her title and journaling on transparencies, then stapled them to her page. This technique gives the page a unique look and can save you time if you don't want to figure out exact text placement before printing.

## MAGGIE'S TOP 5 FONTS
### FOR HERITAGE-THEMED PAGES

• Alte Haas Grotesk
• Bernhard Modern
• Fairfax Station
• Nauert
• Warnock Pro

Warnock Pro is available at *www.myfonts.com*.
All other fonts are available at *www.dafont.com*.

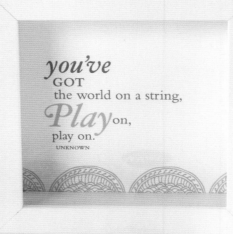

**"YOU'VE GOT THE WORLD ON A STRING" GIFT SET** *by Nicole LaRue*

HOW cool! Set a favorite quote in a cool font and use it to create cards, tags, T-shirts and more.

bonus These cool designs are included on this book's CD. Download them as PDF files and use them to create this darling gift set.

## INSTRUCTIONS

**CARDS:** Print and trim to size.

**TAGS:** Print and punch out with 1" circle punch. Use $\frac{1}{8}$" circle punch for the string hole. Add string.

**JOURNAL:** Print cover and add blank inside sheets (trimmed to the finished size). Use a stapler for the saddle stitch.

**T-SHIRT:** Print design (remember, the design is reversed) onto iron-on transfer sheet. Follow iron-on packaging instructions for adhering image to T-shirt.

**FRAMED PRINT:** Print image and trim to match frame size. Assemble in frame.

# nicole larue on creating gifts for the type-lover

WE SAT DOWN WITH NICOLE LARUE TO TALK ABOUT CREATING GIFTS USING TYPE.

**WHEN YOU'RE CREATING A GIFT SET, WHAT FACTORS DO YOU CONSIDER WHEN CHOOSING A FONT?**

I think it comes down to the recipient. If I were giving my dad a gift, the font would be different than if I were giving the same gift to my mom. For example, I'd be more likely to choose a serif or a script typeface for a gift for my mom, but I imagine I'd use a sans-serif typeface for something for my dad.

**WHAT ARE YOUR TOP FIVE FONTS FOR GIFT SETS?**

I don't have a top five for gift sets in particular, but in general, I find myself using Geometric, Baskerville, Din, Hoefler and Helvetica more often than not.

**ARE THERE ANY "TRICKS" FOR MAKING THE FONTS LOOK SO COOL?**

When I work with type, I like variation—not variation as in using multiple typefaces, but variation in sizes and weights. It's much more fun to illustrate with type than it is to just move lines of it around on a page.

**WHAT TYPES OF ITEMS DO YOU LIKE TO INCLUDE IN GIFT SETS?**

I typically include a couple of store-bought items, like a book or a pen or some candy. This helps balance out the hierarchy in most gifts. Once those items are established, I fill it with little things, like ribbon and tags and cards and confetti.

**WHAT EXTRA LITTLE TOUCHES MAKE A GIFT SET COOL?**

It's all in the details. We tend to put each piece in a gift set into a container as is. But adding awesome detail is all about attaching a small tag with some great thread to each item before putting it into the container. It's taking that extra step to make the gift special that makes it cool.

# Outside INFLUENCES

*chapter 2.2*

I've been inspired by many type designers over the years. Some of my early influences were Carol Twombly and Sumner Stone at Adobe. Later, I discovered companies like House Industries, with their "street" fonts, and Emigre, with their "digital" fonts.

Right now, I'm inspired by the designs and typefaces created by Neville Brody (featured on a recent issue of *Time* magazine as an alternate cover design), Erik Speikermann (the master of readable type for directional and transportation signage), and Jonathan Hoefler and Tobias Frere-Jones of Hoefler & Frere-Jones (H&FJ). They've created some of the most visible and mainstream custom typefaces for a variety of companies and publications, including *O, The Oprah Magazine* and *Martha Stewart Living*.

Take a look at the type on products and signage and other places in your world. What typefaces and cool uses of type inspire you? Perhaps you'll see a coffee mug with cool writing on it, or a movie poster, or product packaging, or a magazine ad, or a billboard or website. Use this inspiration to help you choose type for a layout.

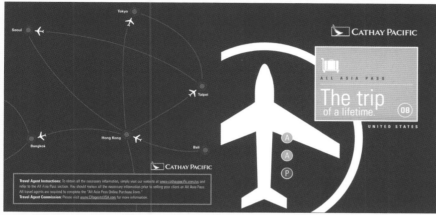

HOW *cool*! Brian used a travel brochure as the inspiration for these three layouts highlighting recent trips. Notice how the bold colors make the white text stand out.

**BROCHURE** *by Cathay Pacific*

## 06 CANCUN

DATE: APRIL 15 - APRIL 22, 2006
DESTINATION: CANCUN, MEXICO
PURPOSE OF VISIT: FAMILY VACATION
NUMBER OF PASSENGERS: 6
ALL-INCLUSIVE: ALL MEALS AND DRINKS!

WE HAD A BIT OF A SCARE A COUPLE OF DAYS BEFORE FLYING OUT. DUE TO THE STORMS THAT DAMAGED MUCH OF CANCUN, WE HAD TO MOVE TO A DIFFERENT HOTEL. THE EL CID THAT WE ENDED UP AT HAD ALL-INCLUSIVE FOOD! THE CHILDREN LOVED THE DAQUIRIS AND PINA COLADAS. RILEY LOVED THE FISH AND ORDERED IT 24 HOURS A DAY. THE HOTEL HAD THE PRETTIEST POOL AND PLAY AREA THAT THE KIDS LOVED TO PLAY IN. THE BEACH WAS CONVENIENTLY LOCATED AND THEY HAD SOME TOYS TO USE OUT THERE. WE WENT ON A COUPLE OF EXCURSIONS, ONE TO EXCARET, TO VISIT THE JUNGLES OF MEXICO. RILEY AND I LOVED TO SNORKEL AND SEE THE FISH UNDER THE WATER. ELLIE AND MIA PREFERRED TO JUST STAY ON THE BEACHES AND PLAY IN THE SAND. WE HAD A FUN TIME VISITING CANCUN IN 2006.

**06 CANCUN** *by Brian Tippetts*

"I'm the **TYPE OF TRAVELER** that takes a ton of vacation pictures. Going to Europe was no exception—I came home with hundreds of pictures from the trip. I used this **16-PHOTO LAYOUT** format to manage the large number of photos and added travel dingbats to reinforce the **VISUAL THEME** of the pages." —*brian tippetts*

**07 EUROPE** *by Brian Tippetts*

"While traveling through airports, you always see the 'ARRIVAL/DEPARTURES' displays that give updated FLIGHT INFORMATION. I thought this look would be a PERFECT FIT for my vacation pages and chose the font Bubbledot to convey that digital-information feel." ——*brian tippetts*

# 08 TOKYO

DATE: FEBRUARY 28 - MARCH 4, 2008
DESTINATION: IKEBEKURU, TOKYO, JAPAN
PURPOSE OF VISIT: CKU JAPAN 2008
NUMBER OF PASSENGERS: 1
MISSING ITEMS: (1) LUGGAGE LOST

I ARRIVED ON A SUNNY AFTERNOON AT THE TOYKO AIRPORT. I FIRST REPORTED MY LOST LUGGAGE. THEN BOARDED THE AIRPORT TRANSPORTATION TO THE HOTEL. TOKYO IS A BIG CITY THAT GOES ON AND ON. THE BUILDINGS ARE GREY AND NON-DESCRIPT BUT THE CITY IS VERY CLEAN. THE CKU-JAPAN TEAM WAS VERY POLITE AND WELCOMING AND WE GOT TOGETHER THE FIRST NIGHT AT A MEXICAN RESTAURANT TO KICK OFF THE EVENT. MY LECTURE TOPIC WAS "SCRAPBOOKING FOR A CAUSE" AND ALL STUDENTS ATTENDED IT. EVEN THOUGH I COMMUNICATED THROUGH A JAPANESE TRANSLATOR, THE MAJORITY OF THE 200+ STUDENTS AND TEACHERS WERE IN TEARS AND WANTED TO DO SOMETHING GOOD FOR OTHERS. I WAS PLEASANTLY SURPRISED AND I WILL NEVER FORGET THE GOOD TIMES ON THIS TRIP.

**08 TOKYO** *by Brian Tippetts*

"My influence for this page was Making Memories' green square logo. I used a **SKETCHIER MONOGRAM** since this is a kid-themed page, but I stuck with a very plain and simple **SANS-SERIF** font for everything else. To create the 'logo' title block, I reversed out the type and printed on white cardstock." —*amanda probst*

Just Micah.

Modeling a shirt Grandma Nancy made for Nathan back when he was two years old.

Carrying on a tradition...while howling in the front yard.

Perfectly delighted with himself, as usual.

September 13, 2007

**micah**moments

**MICAH MOMENTS** *by Amanda Probst*

**making**memories

**LOGO** *by Making Memories*

"This layout was inspired by a **PIECE OF ARTWORK** titled 'And What's the Truth? The Gate of Antoni Gaudi's La Sagrada Familia, Barcelona, Spain' by Bel Phos. I **REPEATED THE PHRASE** 'I love you' in six different languages across the background of the layout. To make one line of text **MORE PROMINENT**, I gradient-faded the other text blocks into the background." —*amy martin*

**I LOVE YOU** *by Amy Martin*

HOW cool! Notice how Amy used bold, simple fonts for her title and journaling to contrast with the script background of her page.

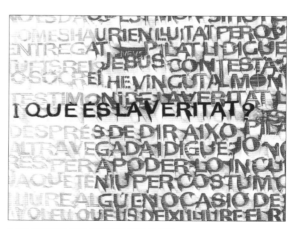

AND WHAT'S THE TRUTH? THE GATE OF ANTONI GAUDI'S LA SAGRADA FAMILIA, BARCELONA, SPAIN *by Bel Phos*

"I love the thin OUTLINED TITLE on my inspiration piece, a
John Coltrane CD. I chose a similarly bold font, Impact, for my
TITLE and subtitle." ——*deena wuest*

**OFFICIALLY MOBILE** *by Deena Wuest*

HOW cool ! Love the look of outlined titles? Try this:

① Choose your font and type your title in Photoshop.
Adjust the spacing until the letters are close or touching.

② After simplifying the layer, select "Edit" then "Stroke."
Under "Stroke," set the width, the color and the location.
(For this page, Deena set the width at 10 px, the color to
white, and the location to "Outside.")

③ Using the Magic Wand tool, select the original text and
hit delete. What you have left is a custom outlined title.

TIP: Another option is to use the Outline Effect in the
Styles and Effects palette or use an outline font, but you
won't achieve this exact result with the letters blending into
each other.

**ONE DOWN, ONE UP: LIVE AT THE HALF NOTE**
*by John Coltrane, Impulse Records*

**MY FOREVER** *by Elizabeth Kartchner*

"I love the MONOCHROMATIC COLORS and the bold title of this card! For my page, I used Boris Black Bloxx for my title because it MATCHES THE FONT on the card, and 2Peas Sailboat for the journaling. I journaled DIRECTLY ON THE PHOTO to keep the simple, clean monochromatic look I was going for."

—*elizabeth Kartchner*

**"FOR LIKE EVER" CARD** *by Village*

"I was INSPIRED BY the mix of fonts and the monochromatic look on the cup from Corner Bakery Café, which led me to try the white stickers on the white cardstock. I like how the CHAOTIC MIX of words and fonts work because of the subtlety of the tone-on-tone look." —*Kelly Purkey*

**RACLETTE DAY** *by Kelly Purkey*

HOW *cool*! Want to try this cool tone-on-tone look with other products? Use letter stamps and a watermark inkpad, like VersaMark from Tsukineko.

**CUP** *by Corner Bakery Café*

M, L & C *by Laura Kurz*

"This **NOTEBOOK FEATURES** a large serif font in a grid and a damask image. I wanted my page to have that same look, so I **PLACED INDIVIDUAL** American Crafts stickers in their own blocks. I love how **THEY'RE SEPARATE** but work together to form the page's title." —*Laura Kurz*

**COMPOSITION BOOK** *by See Jane Work*

"I got my inspiration for this page from an envelope I received in the mail—I really liked the PATTERNED BLOCK LETTERS. Although the letters on the envelope have multiple patterns, I used JUST ONE PATTERN for a less busy look that doesn't distract from the rest of the page." ——*maggie holmes*

JANUARY 2008 *by Maggie Holmes*

HOW *cool!* Follow Maggie's lead and customize your chipboard letters. Choose a bold chipboard font and paint it. After the paint dries, stamp a pattern on each letter. For a different look, try stamping smaller words, letters or images.

"GENIUS" ENVELOPE *by Citi*

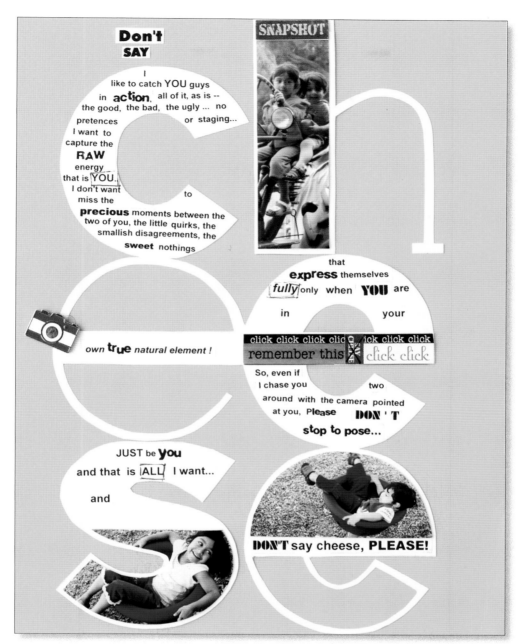

**Don't SAY** c h

SNAPSHOT

I like to catch YOU guys in **action**, all of it, as is -- the good, the bad, the ugly ... no pretences or staging... I want to capture the **RAW** energy that is YOU. I don't want to miss the **precious** moments between the two of you, the little quirks, the smallish disagreements, the **sweet** nothings

that **express** themselves *fully* only when **YOU** are in your

own **true** natural element !

click click click clic k ick click click remember this click click

So, even if I chase you two around with the camera pointed at you, Please **DON'T stop to pose...**

JUST be **you** and that is ALL I want... and

**DON'T say cheese, PLEASE!**

**DON'T SAY CHEESE** *by Mou Saha*

"I chose a mix of fonts so I could EMPHASIZE single words or sections of my journaling. The Arial and Futura fonts make it EASY TO READ while BlueNorma adds a touch of whimsy." — mou saha

**THE CHEESE STANDS ALONE** *by Alexander Isley*

# Text as DESIGN

*chapter 2.3*

In my junior year of college, I had an English course that involved a lot of writing. I found myself behind on a number of papers and had to figure out a way to spruce them up for the teacher's assistant (TA) who would be grading them.

To help, I decided to add some "design flair" to my papers. For example, on a paper about my favorite pastime (surfing), I formatted my text in a wave pattern. Much to my delight, the papers came back with notes from the TA saying, "How did you do this?" or "Wow, that's amazing!" Though most of the time she was referring to the text design and not the content of the paper, I received an A in the class. The lesson? Presentation counts!

After you've written your title or journaling, consider taking an extra step and adding some design flair to your text. A fun way to do this is to fill a shaped space with text. Check out the following pages, then try this look on one of your own layouts.

"I wanted to use the number '8' as a STRONG ELEMENT on the page, but I didn't want it to overwhelm my photos. Adding the text along a path VISUALLY CREATES the '8' and still allows the pictures of Mia to stand out." —brian tippetts

**IT IS GREAT TO BE 8** *by Brian Tippetts*

HOW cool! You can try this look too! Type paths for numbers 0–9 are included on the bonus CD.

"For a fun title block, try CUTTING OUT a basic shape and fitting your words inside it in an interesting way. I just sketched this out with pencil and then went over the OUTLINES with black pen. After erasing my PENCIL MARKS, I added the color. Voilà! The mini letter stickers were perfect for the journaling 'string.'"

—amanda probst

**LET'S GO FLY A KITE** *by Amanda Probst*

HOW cool! If you're not comfortable drawing your own shapes, try using this technique with die cuts.

...............................................

HOW cool! Notice how Amy used words in several places on her card: the background design, the center of the flower, the text strip along the bottom edge and the sentiment above it.

**"CELEBRATE THE EVERYDAY" CARD** *by Amy Martin*

"I wanted to use a good VARIETY OF FONTS on this layout while keeping the overall feeling organized and clean. I chose my favorite font from each of these CATEGORIES: serif, sans serif, slab serif and script. I used one of my favorite things, a Reese's Peanut Butter Cup, as COLOR INSPIRATION for my design." —*Deena Wuest*

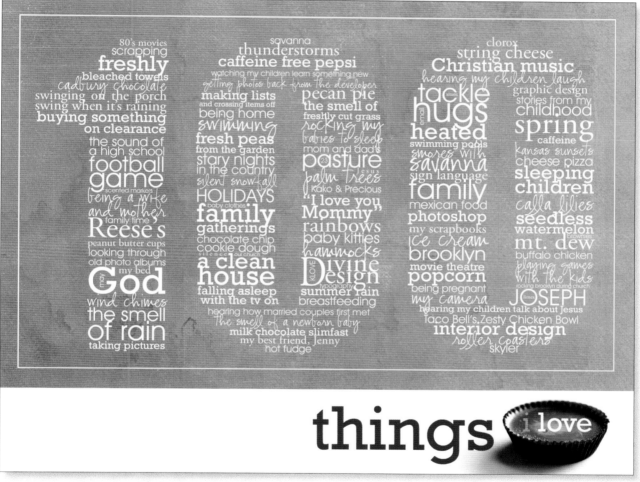

**100 THINGS I LOVE** *by Deena Wuest*

HOW cool! Filling letters and numbers with text looks so cool! Here are Deena's steps for this technique:

① Type your word or numbers on your page (here, Deena typed "100"). Enlarge it to span the length of your canvas.

② Add each line of text in a separate text box and adjust the size and font until it fits nicely inside.

③ When all your text is complete, simply delete the first layer ("100") to create this cool effect.

TIP: You can purchase or download digital templates that are preset—just add your text, and your journaling takes the shape of the template letter, number or shape.

**CHIT CHAT** *by Elizabeth Kartchner*

HOW cool! Elizabeth downloaded a digital brush with the silhouette image of a woman on a cell photo, then filled the image with journaling in a variety of fonts. Because the image is complex, she didn't delete the brush layer after adding her text.

"I chose Old Remington and Uncle Charles because they were in the SAME FONT FAMILY, and I knew they would match up when printed in the same size and layered. I typed lines of the word 'love,' printed them out on patterned paper, then CUT THEM with a circle template. I erased the type and replaced it with lines of the word 'life' in the SAME DOCUMENT so the lines matched up. Then I printed them out and hand-cut the countries." —Kelly Purkey

"WELCOME TO THE WORLD" CARD *by Kelly Purkey*

"On first glance, one might not even notice my son buried deep in the picture, so I **POSITIONED MY JOURNALING** directly on the photo to highlight the path he was walking and to draw attention to him. I **TYPED OUT EACH LINE** of text and slightly increased each one in point size to represent depth of field." —*deena wuest*

**ADVENTURE AWAITS** *by Deena Wuest*

HOW cool! Always try out several type styles on your pages. Deena initially chose a script font for this page about her son, but it felt too formal for the subject matter. Even though the fun, modern feel of this slab-serif font contrasts with the natural look of the photo, it was a better choice overall.

"I drew two DIFFERENT-SIZED pumpkins on cardstock. For the smaller pumpkin, I arranged the word stickers in rows, keeping within the pumpkin outlines. Then I cut out the WHOLE PUMPKIN and divided it into sections. I arranged these pieces on top of the orange pumpkin and traced the OVERLAPPING OUTLINES. After cutting out the orange pumpkin, I stamped my journaling inside it." —mou saha

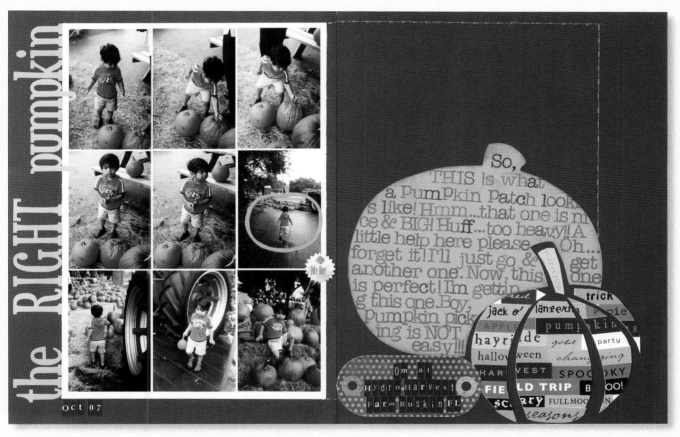

THE RIGHT PUMPKIN *by Mou Saha*

HOW cool! Notice how Mou used the pumpkin shapes on her layout. The large orange pumpkin holds her journaling, while the pumpkin filled with Halloween-themed word stickers serves as a cute page accent.

# Mediums

*chapter 2.4*

When I studied typography for design, I focused mainly on digital fonts. In scrapbooking, however, type mediums include fonts, rub-ons, chipboard, stamps, stickers, pre-printed titles and quotes, die cuts, handwriting and more. We have so many options when it comes to placing letters and words on layouts—and happily, most are customizable.

Take a look at the following ideas for using different type mediums, then pull out the type mediums in your stash—what cool things can you do with them?

"I just love this background stamp for its VISUAL FEAST OF LETTERS. I didn't want to actually use any of the words hidden here, though. Instead, I wanted a fun, carefree card. To BREAK OUT OF THE GRID, I simply handwrote 'hi,' then colored it in a bit with black and yellow glaze pens." —*amanda probst*

..............................................

HOW *cool*! Use your own handwriting to add playful contrast to fonts or stamped letters.

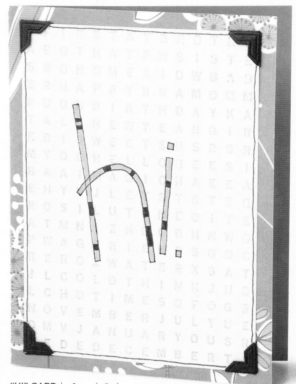

"HI" CARD *by Amanda Probst*

..............................................................................

"I LOVE YOU" CARD *by Maggie Holmes*

"I used **MY HANDWRITING** to create a friendly, loving and playful mood on my card. First, I **STAMPED** the journaling block onto my card to give me a place for **MY WRITING**. Then I used a Slick Writer from American Crafts to write the message." —*maggie holmes*

She never stops watching...
I can see it all processing in her head— wondering what's next. All the while, completely trusting, knowing that she's in good hands. that she is loved and she knows it. That kind of innocent learning that is only possible at this precious age.

I love watching, HER
watching her learn
watching her grow
watching her develop

She's not the only one watching and learning...

WATCH & learn
CAPRI... April '08

**WATCH & LEARN** *by Heidi Swapp*

HOW cool! Notice how Heidi wrote her journaling over patterned paper with a subtle print. The pattern adds visual interest without distracting from the text.

# heidi swapp on including your handwriting on your pages

WE SAT DOWN WITH HEIDI SWAPP TO TALK ABOUT HANDWRITING ON SCRAPBOOK PAGES.

## ON WHAT TYPES OF PAGES DO YOU ABSOLUTELY NEED TO HANDWRITE YOUR JOURNALING?

I use my handwriting on all of my projects. For me, it's much quicker and easier than using the computer for journaling. But I do think it's really nice to use your own handwriting when you're sharing more personal and tender feelings. It adds to the meaning of the sentiments.

## WHY IS IT IMPORTANT TO HANDWRITE ELEMENTS ON YOUR SCRAPBOOK PAGES?

Your handwriting reflects who you are. Whether you like your handwriting or not, it's you—it's like leaving a little piece of you for others to remember and connect with. Think about the people you're close to . . . you can probably picture their handwriting in your mind. It really is a legacy!

## WHAT DO YOU USE DIFFERENT PEN-TIP SIZES FOR?

I like to use different pen-tip sizes on every page I create. Thick tips are perfect for bold, large titles, or for adding emphasis to a word in your journaling, just like using bold print on your computer. I like to use a thin point size, like .5mm or .3mm, when I have a lot to write. The writing looks neater and takes up less space. Using different tips can help you emphasize words, dates, titles, subtitles and even names and places.

## HOW DO YOU MAKE CUTE HANDWRITTEN TITLES?

I have two tips:

① Practice, practice, practice. Just like anything, you need to practice! Write your title out a couple of times on a piece of scratch paper before you begin.

② Always use pencil first. Always! Knowing you can erase mistakes takes the pressure off. And if you don't like the look, just start over!

## WHAT IF YOU MESS UP A WORD OR A LETTER? ARE THERE ANY CLEVER FIXES YOU CAN RECOMMEND?

My typical "mess-up" is a spelling error I don't realize until my husband points it out when my layout is all done. I usually go into "re-creation" mode. I hate that! But I've been known to re-write on a piece of paper and add it over the top of my mistake. That's what "scrap" booking is all about! Remember: pencil first!

Love is a push on the swing
a batch of cookies
a present hidden in a suitcase
walks and painting
made-up games
rock collecting and snuggles.

*Love*

you are
*amazing*

Love is Grandma.

**LOVE** *by Jessica Sprague*

HOW cool! Notice how Jessica colored her text red to reinforce the theme of the page.

## HOW DO YOU CUSTOMIZE A FONT?

I like to add brushes to them! Here's how:

① **CREATE** a new blank document. Select the Horizontal Type tool and choose your font, font size and color in the Options bar at the top of the screen. Type your text.

② **OPEN** a brush file (I used the .png file that came with the brush set). Select the Lasso tool and draw a selection around the area of the brush you would like to use. Type Ctrl-C to copy. Switch over to your new document and type Ctrl-V to paste.

③ **GO TO** Edit > Fill to recolor the brush to the same color as your text (make sure the Preserve Transparency checkbox is checked in the Fill Layer dialog box). Rotate, flip or erase parts of the brush file to attach it to the font. Repeat Steps 2 and 3 for any other portions of the brush you would like to use.

# jessica sprague on customizing fonts

**WE SAT DOWN WITH JESSICA SPRAGUE TO TALK ABOUT CUSTOMIZING FONTS FOR USE ON SCRAPBOOK PAGES.**

### WHAT TYPES OF FONTS WORK WELL FOR THIS TECHNIQUE?

I really like flourishy fonts, like Fling, which I used for this project, or grungy fonts, such as One Fell Swoop—both lend themselves to extra flourishes and hide imperfections in your creation. But it would be an interesting look to juxtapose a very simple font with some flourishes, too.

### WHAT FACTORS DO YOU CONSIDER WHEN CHOOSING A FONT FOR THIS TECHNIQUE?

I try to choose fonts and brushes that have similar lines and curvy shapes, so the addition looks natural. If the font has very thin lines, I'll need a thin brush. If it's a very scripty, ornate font, or a grungy font, I'll need a brush to match it.

### WHAT ARE YOUR FAVORITE FONTS FOR THIS TECHNIQUE?

I really like Fling, enough that I paid $39 for it. But there are plenty of great free options as well. Check out these from *www.dafont.com*:

• Freebooter Script: Perfect for clean-lined ornaments.
• Hawaii Killer: A grungier flourish.

• KissMeKissMeKissMe: Great with doodle or hand-drawn brushes.
• Olho de Boi: Hand-drawn and imperfect.
• One Fell Swoop: Great with ornate brushes.

### HOW ABOUT BRUSHES?

My favorite brushes to add to fonts come from:
• Anna Aspnes at *www.designerdigitals.com*.
• MaryAnn Wise at *www.designerdigitals.com*.
• Nancie Rowe Janitz at *www.scrapartist.com*.
• Rhonna Farrer at *www.twopeasinabucket.com*.

### WHAT ARE SOME OTHER WAYS TO DIGITALLY CUSTOMIZE A TITLE?

• Some fonts come with ornaments as a separate file or as part of the font itself. For example, the Marcelle font comes with a Swash font you can use to add swashes underneath. For the Porcelain font, just type the < and > keys to access the flourishes.

• For more standard fonts, I like to split each letter onto its own layer and then play with the sizing and spacing of the individual letters for more interest.

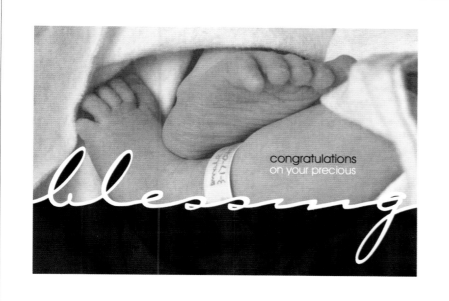

**"BLESSING" CARD** *by Deena Wuest*

"I love the **PEACEFUL** and calm feeling the script font Carpenter **EVOKES**. I thought it was perfect for a card for a new baby. I **PAIRED IT WITH** the sans-serif font Avant Garde to **GIVE** the card an updated, modern look."
—deena wuest

HOW cool! Notice how Deena used the word "blessing" to span the width of the card and act as a divider between her photo and the bottom border.

. . . . . . . . . . . . . . . . . . . . . . . . . . . . . . . . . . . . . . . . . . . . . . . . . . . . . . . . . . . . . . . . . . . . . . . . . . . . . .

"I formed the words 'thanks' to look like SMOKE COMING OUT of the house's chimney. Adding text in curves with a graphics program is a SIMPLE WAY to add a fun touch to a layout or card."
—amy martin

HOW cool! Notice how the typewriter font is a nice contrast to the bold handwritten style of the card's sentiment.

**"THANK YOU" CARD** *by Amy Martin*

"I chose this font because it's a close MATCH TO THE ARTWORK used in the Harry Potter books. To give it a little more dimension on my page, I PRINTED IT IN REVERSE on cardstock and cut it out."

—Kelly Purkey

**HARRY POTTER** *by Kelly Purkey*

HOW cool! Love the font on a popular product or from a favorite movie? You may be able to find it, or a font in a similar style, as an online download.

# heidi swapp on using lettering products

**WE SAT DOWN WITH HEIDI SWAPP TO TALK ABOUT USING LETTERING PRODUCTS ON SCRAPBOOK PAGES.**

**WHAT'S YOUR FAVORITE TYPE OF LETTERING PRODUCT TO USE?**

I love to use black pens for journaling. I love to use different tip sizes, especially when they're brand-new! I always like to have a gray pen for shadowing my lettering, too.

**HOW DO YOU LIKE TO USE LETTERING PRODUCTS ON YOUR PAGES?**

I love to mix the point sizes of my pens and vary my lettering styles. I also love to mix my handwriting with stamped letters.

**HOW DO YOU CHOOSE LETTERING PRODUCTS FOR A SCRAPBOOK PAGE?**

I choose products based on what I want to say, and how much room I have to say it.

**HOW CAN YOU CUSTOMIZE LETTERING PRODUCTS TO FIT YOUR PAGES?**

• Alter the color using paints or inks.
• Add chipboard letters, stamps or letter stickers to your handwritten elements.
• "Frame" your titles and journaling with paper, printed frames, stamps and more.

**TRAVEL HIGHLIGHTS** *by Heidi Swapp*

HOW cool! Notice how Heidi mixed her handwriting with rub-on letters to create a cool page title.

**HOW cool!** Letter stickers are available in a wonderful selection of colors and textures. Choose a textured variety to add extra visual interest to your scrapbook page or card.

**"THANK YOU" CARD** *by Kelly Purkey*

"Using **GLITTER STICKERS** and a cursive font makes this card ultra girlie." ——*kelly purkey*

"I chose a mixed style of chipboard letters, stickers and stamps to reflect the CHEERFUL MOOD of this card." —— *mou saha*

HOW cool! Add small letter stickers to larger chipboard letters to create an additional layer of meaning for your card sentiment or page title.

**"THANK U" CARD** *by Mou Saha*

A PLACE WE CALL HOME *by Laura Kurz*

"I wanted a title that had impact and LOVED THE WAY THE COLOR and simple style of these acetate letters go with the beach feel of the page. I used the SERIF FONT Times New Roman for the journaling to contrast with the sans-serif title."

—Laura Kurz

# Style
## FUN

chapter 2.5

There's more to type than just upper- and lowercase letters, numerals and a few punctuation marks. More advanced fonts include ligatures (combined characters), accent characters (Latin languages), old-style numerals, dingbats, and options like uppercase and lowercase alternates that have a "swash" feel to them.

These extras lend even more versatility to great fonts. Speaking of versatility, we've included ideas on how to get a variety of looks from a single font. Read on for more tips for choosing the right font and pointers for mixing typefaces.

1 FONT, 3 LOOKS

We asked Elizabeth, Laura and Mou to each
create a page using the American Typewriter
font. Take a look at all three pages to see how
versatile a single typeface can be.

**8 A.M.** *by Elizabeth Kartchner*

HOW cool! Notice how Elizabeth's journaling box doubles as a photo mat.

"I wanted to make a **BIG STATEMENT** with the title, so I made the '1' huge! I used a much smaller font size to journal around the cluster of **PHOTOGRAPHS** on the second page." ——*Laura Kurz*

**CAMDEN TURNS ONE** *by Laura Kurz*

HOW cool! Laura used a small charm to mark the beginning of her journaling. She emphasized the understated nature of her text by using all lowercase letters.

"I varied the **SIZE, WEIGHT, STYLE AND COLOR** of the American Typewriter font to emphasize the title and certain sections of the text. I **ROTATED** the textbox at an angle for a fun effect." ——*mou saha*

**UH OH, THAT WASN'T SUPPOSED TO HAPPEN!** *by Mou Saha*

HOW *cool*! Mou gave this font a workout! Notice how varied the text looks even though she only used one typeface.

**BEHIND THE LENS** *by Maggie Holmes*

## TYPE MAKEOVER

Even though a typeface may be cute, sometimes it's just not a good choice for a layout. Take a look at these two pages to see how a type makeover enhances the overall look of the layout.

### << BEFORE

This script features tall, loopy ascenders that crisscross over into other letters, making for a visually complex, difficult-to-read title. The journaling font is extremely formal, and doesn't suit the casual nature of the page. It's also difficult to read at this size.

"Fancy SCRIPT FONTS are nice, but in this case the font ISN'T READABLE and doesn't fit the style of the page."
—*maggie holmes*

### AFTER >>

This sans-serif title is bold and easy to read, even at a small size. The journaling font is also a simple sans-serif font that suits the casual nature of the page and is easy to read.

"I CHOSE Impact for my title because I wanted it to be bold and STAND OUT. I chose Geneva for my journaling because it's a CLEAN, modern font that's easy to read."
—*maggie holmes*

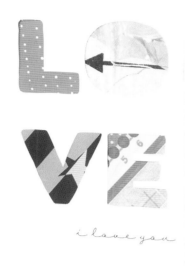

## MIX & MATCH TYPE

Can you use more than one typeface on a page and still have an eye-pleasing look? You bet you can! We asked Amy and Elizabeth to use multiple typefaces on a single project. Take a look at the results!

"I chose these fonts because I LOVE THE MIX of the bold font with the cutesy cursive font. To create colorful LETTERS LIKE the word 'Love,' just cut out the letters using an X-acto knife, then back them with different PATTERNED PAPERS." —*elizabeth Kartchner*

"LOVE" CARD *by Elizabeth Kartchner*

"Picking and choosing fonts that MESH WELL together is important. Here, I chose different fonts for the various WORDS IN THE QUOTE. I adjusted the placement of the words to help draw the viewer in." —*amy martin*

## MIX & MATCH TYPE TIPS

① Use contrasting type styles. Choosing same-style typefaces won't create enough contrast to make the piece visually interesting (it will just look like you forgot to put everything in the same typeface).

② Two typefaces or four type variations (size, bold, italics, etc.) is plenty!

③ Play with size or color or style of the typeface if you want more visual variety within your text. You can also change the thickness (weight), apply italics or reverse out the type.

④ Don't change typefaces within a paragraph—use bold or italics for emphasis.

⑤ Prevent clunky-looking text blocks by choosing variable-width typefaces over mono-spaced typefaces (where every character is the same width).

EVERY FLOWER *by Amy Martin.*

# COOL
# TECHNIQUES

# Section THREE

**I LOVE LOOKING THROUGH** magazines and coming across ads or feature openers that use type in fun, interesting ways. It's fascinating to see cool effects and techniques using type as the medium.

Early on at *Creating Keepsakes*, I designed a birth announcement for Lisa Bearnson. She and I have children born the same year, and she had seen some announcements I had created. I was amazed by the response when she featured my design, which spelled out her baby's name in letter blocks, in her Editor's Note. Several readers called in wanting me to create their birth announcements, too. Knowing how to manipulate type is a powerful design tool!

Check out the cool type techniques on the following pages, then try one of these ideas on your next layout.

# PROJECT to Page

*chapter* 3.1

We asked each of our magazine designers to create a cool typography project for our page designers to use as inspiration for a card or scrapbook layout. The assignment was simple: Be as creative as you want and use type as your focus. After a few days, I started seeing the beginnings of some very cool work. When all was completed, they had successfully created unique projects that use type in interesting ways.

The next step was having our page designers translate the type ideas from these projects onto cards or scrapbook pages. Once again, their creativity went beyond my expectations. I think you'll find both the inspiration pieces and the layouts amazing! Check out the following pages, then take the challenge yourself—choose an inspiration piece and see what you can do with type.

**BLUE ALPHABET** *by Brian Tippetts*

"I'm always fascinated by letter-forms—both INDIVIDUALLY and as a group. This typeface, Perla, provides some very INTERESTING SHAPES with the 'bulbs,' the thick and thins, and the letter variations."
—brian tippetts

HOW cool! This engaging alphabet background uses repetition to draw the eye to the single character printed in a different color.

"I wanted the typeface to be MASCULINE but FUN for this new baby boy card."
—laura kurz

HOW cool! Laura not only borrowed the blue background from Brian's alphabet, but she also used the repeated letters in the inspiration piece to emphasize her message. This is a great way to use up leftover letter stickers.

**"OH BOY" CARD** *by Laura Kurz*

**"NAME THAT FONT" GAME** *by Erin Bayless*

HOW cool! Check out this darling font identification game! Erin's font picks are diverse, yet they all work well together visually.

"I chose **FUN, DISTINCTIVE FONTS** that started with the letters of my title (the P is Pegsanna, the S is Sketch Rockwell and the A is Alba). Yes, I know that choosing a font that started with the **SAME INITIAL** wasn't really necessary, but it actually helped immensely in narrowing down my **CHOICES** so I could just decide!" —*amanda probst*

**PSA** *by Amanda Probst*

HOW cool! Amanda positioned the staggered title letters and changed the type colors using Adobe InDesign, then applied Glossy Accents on top to add a bit more dimension. For the journaling block, she used InDesign to create a square with rounded corners that mimics her photo shapes (and the shape of Erin's cards) and typed her text inside it. She selected Text Wrap and inverted the wrapping so it wrapped inside the shape instead of around it.

**"BUTTERFLY" CARD** *by Janice Barfuss*

HOW cool! At first glance, you might just see a stylized butterfly shape, but look closer—the entire design is created with individual letters! The swirly font suits the subject matter perfectly.

"I selected these stickers because of their COLORS—together they were perfect for CREATING A TREE." —— mou saha

plant · water · sprout · feed · bloom · enjoy.

pLant a 👜 & watch it GROW

**WATCH IT GROW** *by Mou Saha*

HOW cool ! When constructing her alphabet tree, Mou used loopy letters on the edges and then filled in the tree, leaving space for the trunk and branches.

HOW cool! Natalie's heartfelt T-shirt design combines text and silhouette shapes in a series of repeated rectangles.

**"SAVE OUR PLANET" T-SHIRT** *by Natalie Reich*

HOW cool! Following Natalie's design, Elizabeth included simple words and images inside the squares. She cut around the foam shapes in each square to really make them stand out.

**"WISH YOU WERE HERE" CARD** *by Elizabeth Kartchner*

"I loved PAIRING THE SCRIPTY FONT with the typewritten font, and creating a title that filled the whole page." —*Laura Kurz*

**YOU ARE LOVED** *by Laura Kurz*

HOW cool! Laura kept the type in the same vertical space on each of the three rectangles but alternated sides to keep the title flowing down the page.

"YOUR WORDS" CARDS *by Nicole LaRue*

HOW cool! In true hip and handmade style, Nicole used playful handwritten
type variations to convey a poignant message.

"For this layout, I had FUN PLAYING with a new technique: changing a bold font into an outline font." —elizabeth Kartchner

**DAILY ROUTINE** *by Elizabeth Kartchner*

HOW cool! Like Nicole, Elizabeth focused her project on the idea of awakening to a new day. Notice how she also emulated random yet repeated font choices similar to the original design.

# Digital TYPE TECHNIQUES

*chapter 3.2*

When I was first introduced to *The Photoshop WOW! Book*, I was mesmerized by the remarkable tips and tricks I discovered. Technology has taken typography to incredible new places, and now it's easier than ever to do fantastic feats with type. From using type on a path to making titles look 3-D to adding a layer of text to a photo, there are so many cool possibilities. And best of all, these techniques look amazing on scrapbook pages!

In this chapter, we asked our designers to use a fun digital-type technique on their pages. Read on to see their cool ideas, and be sure to try typing on a path—we've included step-by-step instructions and ready-to-use type paths on the bonus CD included with this book.

"My daughter, at only TWO YEARS OLD, had already developed quite the little personality! I couldn't resist using this photo of her playing with her pink superstar glasses, and I knew I wanted the TYPOGRAPHY TO REFLECT the happy, LIVELY MOOD of her expression. The Peach Fuzz font matches the spontaneous fun and playful nature of this photo." —*brian tippetts*

**MY LITTLE ELLIE** *by Brian Tippetts*

HOW *cool*! Brian created type paths in Adobe Illustrator to give the type a fun wavy shape that conveys his daughter's happy, carefree nature.

"One of my **FAVORITE TECHNIQUES** is using my own text to create custom patterned paper. To achieve this look, I duplicate key words from my journaling to use as a background. I then **ENLARGE, LAYER,** recolor and adjust the opacity on each word until I achieve the look I want." —*deena Wuest*

**SUBMIT. PRAY. CELEBRATE. REPEAT.** *by Deena Wuest*

**HOW cool!** This entire layout was created with Photoshop and a single font. No elements, no papers—just photos and words. To add subtle interest to the title, Deena copied a portion of her photo (the water) and used it to fill the word "repeat."

"I chose this font because it feels VERY CRISP and classic to me. I think it MATCHES the tall trees in the photos." —*Kelly Purkey*

**BEAUTIFUL COLORS** *by Kelly Purkey*

HOW cool! Did you notice that Kelly layered text into her photo?
You can replicate her technique:
1. Using Photoshop, add layers of white text onto your photo.
2. Reduce the opacity of the text so that most of the photo can be seen through the letters.
3. Duplicate the background layer (the photo) and place it on top of all of the text layers.
4. Use the Eraser tool to erase the photo where you want the text to show through so that some of the edges blend into the photo.
5. Flatten all layers.

**SUSHI LOVE** *by Elizabeth Kartchner*

"Journaling in the **SHAPE OF HEARTS** goes right along with the title and concept of my layout." —*elizabeth Kartchner*

I had never tasted or even tried a bite of sushi until after I married Collin. The thought of raw fish was very unappetizing to me. But he loved it and convinced me to give it a try. Not only did I like it. I absolutely love it. And we eat it all the time now. yummy!

If there is a special occasion or something to celebrate you know where to find the fam- together at Happy Sumo.

Our favorite sushi restaurant is Happy Sumo! And some of our favorite rolls are the Firecracker. Vegas Roll, baked scallop California Roll. Playboy Roll. and the Dragon Roll. Mmmmm! With a side of tempera veggies please! This is definitely making me hungry! This past year we went as a family on Christmas Eve. 2007

HOW cool! The Paint Bucket tool in Photoshop allows you to color certain areas of your text. Elizabeth used it to highlight overlapping areas in her title letters and color them red.

In addition, she drew attention to the letters L-O-V-E in the alphabet block by printing them red and cutting out heart shapes around each letter in the word.

**I LOVE YOU** *by Jessica Sprague*

. . . . . . . . . . . . . . . . . . . . . . . . . . . . . . . . . . . . . . . . . . . . . . . . . . . . . . . . .

HOW cool! Jessica created a wavy type path for her journaling to represent flower stems on her layout.

bonus! This cool type path is included on this book's CD. Download it to use with Photoshop Elements. Here's how to use it:

① Create a new blank document that's either the size of your layout or the size of your journaling block. Open the *JS-CurvingTextPaths.psd* file on the CD.

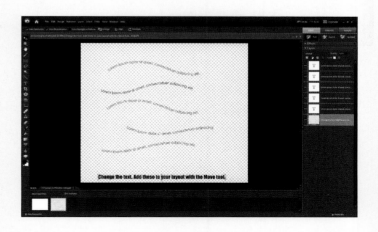

# jessica sprague on curving text

WE SAT DOWN WITH JESSICA SPRAGUE TO TALK ABOUT TYPE PATHS ON SCRAPBOOK PAGES.

### WHAT ARE YOUR TIPS FOR KEEPING THE TEXT LEGIBLE WHEN IT'S IN A PATH?

I don't recommend using a script font for curving paths, especially ones with a dramatic curve, because the text becomes very difficult to read. Keep the font simple.

### WHAT SHAPES WORK BEST FOR TEXT PATHS?

Text paths come in two basic varieties: Type that fills a shape, such as a circle, and type that traces along a shape, such as a curve or a spiral. You can find premade text paths in all kinds of shapes at online digital shops.

### IS THERE AN IDEAL FONT SIZE FOR TEXT IN PATHS?

I wouldn't recommend anything below 12 points.

### WHAT TYPES OF FONTS WORK BEST WITH TEXT PATHS?

It depends on whether you're creating journaling or accent text. For multiple lines of journaling, I rely on a simple serif font (such as Palatino or Times New Roman) or sans-serif font (such as Century Gothic or Gill Sans) to keep the text as readable as possible. For accent text, which is as much about decoration as it is about legibility, I might choose a font with a little more interest, such as Daydream from Fonthead Design.

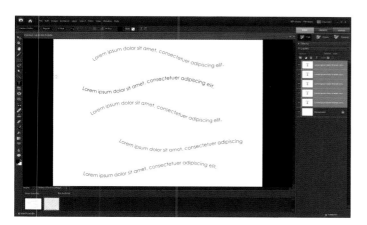

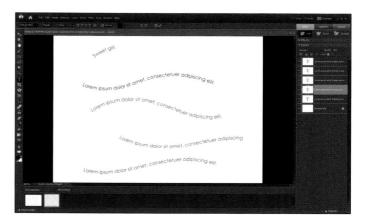

② Select the Move tool. Uncheck the Auto Select Layer checkbox in the Options bar. Hold down Shift while you click on the top layer in the Layers palette, and then on the bottom type layer to select all the type layers. Click and drag the type layers down onto the thumbnail of your layout in the Project Bin. Click and drag the lines into position, then recheck the Auto Select Layer checkbox.

③ Select the Horizontal Type tool. Click on the top journaling line, delete the placeholder text and type your journaling on the lines. Use the options in the Options bar to change the font, color and size of your text. Note that the text will not wrap onto the next curved line—you'll need to click on the next line to change the text and continue your journaling.

# HYBRID TYPE *Techniques*

One of the best things about scrapbooking is the array of options available when it comes to type. Fonts, letter stickers, stamps, rub-ons, chipboard, die cuts and other lettering products provide so many opportunities to customize page titles, journaling blocks and more.

I love to see how creative and cool type can be when digital elements are combined with traditional scrapbooking products on scrapbook pages. We gave our designers this challenge, and the pages they created are pure fun! Pull out your favorite fonts and scrapbooking products, then use them together to create a stylish look on your next page.

"If you're going to HAND-STITCH your title, make sure to choose a large font!" —amy martin

EYES *by Amy Martin*

HOW cool! You can combine digital and traditional scrapbooking easily. Like Amy, design your layout on the computer and print it out (except for the title) on a piece of cardstock. Then print your title, cut it out and stitch it directly to the layout for extra textural interest.

"You can **MANIPULATE** text to fit your layout's theme. I shifted the entire phrase 'Then & Now' to appear as sound coming out of the **DINOSAUR'S** open mouth." —— *mou saha*

Nini saw dinosaurs for the first time in the movie *Jurassic Park* and had been phobic of them ever since. No amount of reassurance convinced her that she is safe as dinos are long gone.

I was quite taken aback when recently she expressed interest in visiting MOSI to see a special dinosaur exhibit. Unsure of what to expect from Nini, we went to MOSI. She walked in with her head high, read the plaques carefully, participated in the interactives bravely and even watched a very realistic "Dinosaurs Alive" in the IMAX Dome Theater without blinking. At the end, she even asked me to buy her a couple of simple books about dinosaurs and a faux dino fossil tile .

On our way home, she said, "Mommy, I will do dinosaurs for show and tell when school starts. I'll show my friends how they used to be and how they are now... okay?" "Absolutely Nini", I managed to say, overwhelmed with pride and joy that my little girl faced her fears and learned from the experience. Yeah Baby, you are ready to take on the world, NOW!!!

**DINOSAURS THEN & NOW** *by Mou Saha*

HOW cool! Mou's layout seamlessly incorporates both computer and hand-crafting. She digitally stitched her photos together and layered text across them. For the title, she used acetate letters as masks, slightly overlapping them and tracing around them with a pen. She added brown and orange alcohol ink to a couple of the letters and adhered them over the traced letters.

**365 DAYS** *by Deena Wuest*

HOW cool! Deena wanted to play off the cool squiggle paper, so she typed her title numerous times in different fonts and used the outline feature in Photoshop to create this incredible green-on-white design. Try it yourself!

① Use the Horizontal Type tool to add your text.

② In the Layers and Effects palette, select Effects/All.

③ Click and drag the Medium Outline effect directly on top of your text to create each outline.

④ Copy your entire project and change the outlines to white, and the background to black. Print out both copies.

⑤ Adhere the black-and-white print onto cardboard numbers, trimming around each one with a craft knife.

⑥ Carefully line the numbers up on your layout to create a seamless design.

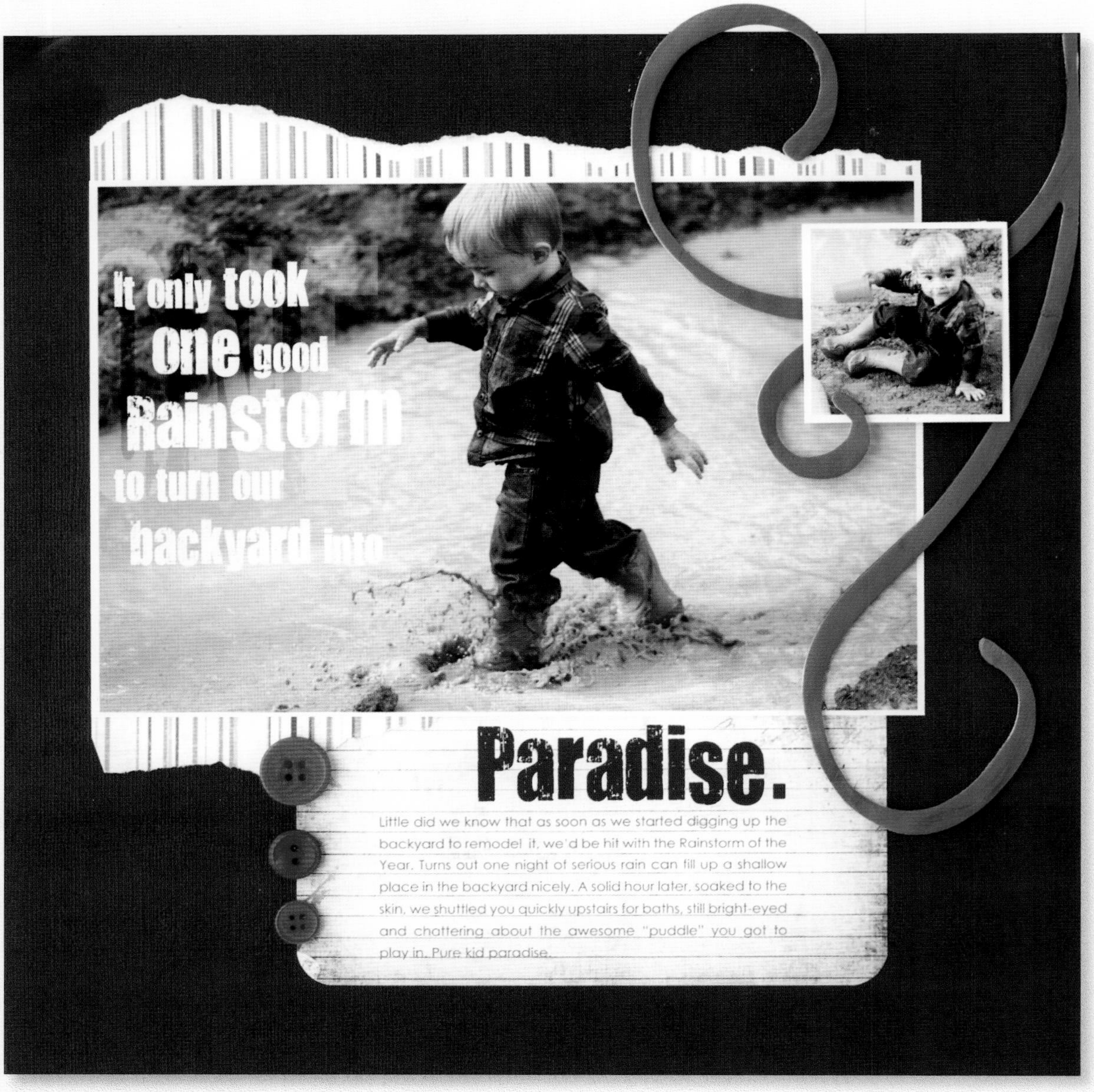
It only took
one good
Rainstorm
to turn our
backyard into
Paradise.
Little did we know that as soon as we started digging up the backyard to remodel it, we'd be hit with the Rainstorm of the Year. Turns out one night of serious rain can fill up a shallow place in the backyard nicely. A solid hour later, soaked to the skin, we shuttled you quickly upstairs for baths, still bright-eyed and chattering about the awesome "puddle" you got to play in. Pure kid paradise.

**PARADISE** *by Jessica Sprague*

HOW cool! Before you print your photo, add a title, a photo caption, a quote or a small amount of journaling to it. Here, Jessica shows you how:

① Open the photo you'd like to add text to. Crop it to the size you'll be printing it, or add it to a letter-sized document.

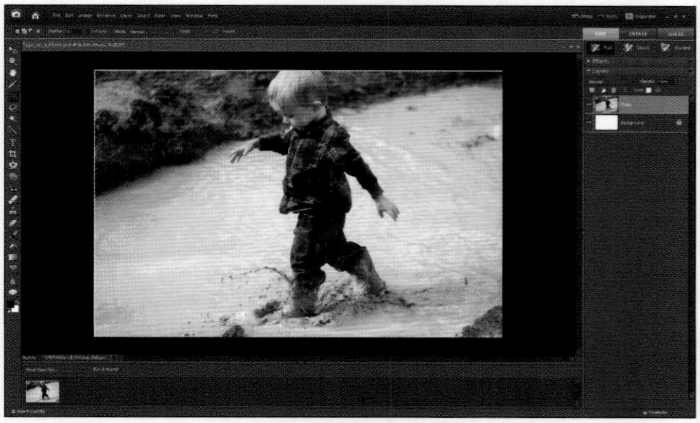

# jessica sprague on adding text to photos

WE SAT DOWN WITH JESSICA SPRAGUE TO TALK ABOUT ADDING TEXT TO PHOTOS BEFORE ADDING THEM TO SCRAPBOOK PAGES.

**WHAT FACTORS DO YOU CONSIDER WHEN ADDING TEXT TO A PHOTO?**

① I always choose a photo where the subject is off-center. This leaves me free to use the remaining photo space for type and doesn't distract from the subject.

② I like to choose a photo where the subject is facing in toward the empty space on the photo. This helps the type and the photo subject work together.

**IS THERE ANYTHING YOU DO WITH THIS TECHNIQUE TO ENHANCE READABILITY?**

Because I almost always use this technique as the title of my layout, I'll typically use a very large font so that any shapes in the photo background won't create visual confusion with the type.

**WHAT TIPS DO YOU HAVE FOR KEEPING THE TEXT FROM DISTRACTING FROM THE SUBJECT OF THE PHOTO?**

① I typically use either black, dark brown or white for my font colors for maximum readability.

② If the photo background is fairly solid, I'll experiment with the opacity of the type as well to help it blend in.

③ If the background of your photo is very busy, consider adding a semi-transparent white rectangle behind your type to help set it off from the photo background.

**ARE THERE CERTAIN TYPES OF FONTS YOU PREFER TO USE FOR THIS TECHNIQUE?**

I like using more decorative fonts for titles, and typing on a photo is no exception. I also like fonts that have some structure to them but also have some added interest, such as You Are Loved, which I used for this page.

② Select the Horizontal Type tool. Change the options in the Options bar at the top of the screen for font, size and color. To type each line of text on its own layer, type one line, then hold down Shift while you click down on the place where you'd like the new line of type to go. Repeat for all additional lines of type.

③ Select the Move tool. Move the lines of type in relationship to each other. With the Horizontal Type tool, select some of the words to change their size.

"I chose the title font for its **SLIGHTLY DISTRESSED** look and its bulk; I wanted something that would fill up the space—not just sit there **SURROUNDED** by layout." —*amanda probst*

**ANCORA IMPARO** *by Amanda Probst*

HOW cool! When you can't find enough of the letters you need, try Amanda's solution: Mix computer-generated fonts with lettering products like chipboard and stickers. *Tip:* Be sure to leave spaces for the lettering products. When Amanda creates the font portion of her title, she actually types letters to stand in for the lettering products. Before printing, she changes the color of those letters to white so they don't print but maintain correct spacing for the lettering products she'll add later on.

"I love using Garamond for journaling; it's a CLASSIC and easy-to-read font. Though the Doodlebug stickers are a much different style, the TWO WORK WELL together." —— *Laura Kurz*

**LOVE FAMILY** *by Laura Kurz*

HOW cool! Laura left spaces in her journaling text to allow room for the title stickers. Notice how she also increased the leading to leave enough vertical space for the letter stickers.

On HaLlOwEEn NiGHT all tHEse Jack o laNTErNs lit OUr Way as wE wENt Trick or trEatiNG in tHE nEigHborhood

**JACK O LANTERNS** *by Mou Saha*

"I used letter stickers to SPELL OUT my journaling, keeping it aligned on the right. In order to make the title stand out, I painted it ORANGE with a glaze pen." ——*mou saha*

HOW cool! In order to create the wiggly, spooky captions, Mou used the Warp function in Photoshop to create different styles of distortion on her letters. Notice the dramatic effect of the white lettering and how she mixed upper- and lowercase letter stickers in her journaling for a cool, quirky look.

# *Traditional* TYPE TECHNIQUES

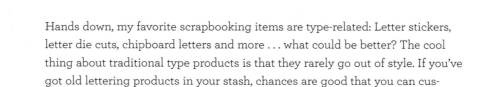

Hands down, my favorite scrapbooking items are type-related: Letter stickers, letter die cuts, chipboard letters and more . . . what could be better? The cool thing about traditional type products is that they rarely go out of style. If you've got old lettering products in your stash, chances are good that you can customize them to give them a fresh, current look.

Take a look at the following pages for inspiring ideas you can use with your traditional type products.

**PRETTY GIRL** *by Maggie Holmes*

HOW **cool**! Get more out of your die-cut and chipboard letters. If you don't have letters in the color you need, line the letters up on your page (without adhering them) and trace around them with a marker. When you lift them off, you'll have a custom title—and you'll still have the letters to use on another project!

"Add **RUB-ONS** to your title letters for a cute effect."
—maggie holmes

...........................................

HOW **cool**! To create the textured title, Amy glued seed beads to her plain paper letters. She also applied beads to the flowers to create unity in her design. Consider other ways you can dress up hand-cut, die-cut or chipboard letters:

- Ink or paint the edges or the entire front of the letter.
- Adhere glitter for sparkle.
- Add embossing powder for shine.
- Apply large flourishy rub-ons to add beautiful detail.

**UP YOU GO** *by Amy Martin*

"I chose SP Purkalator because it's kind of a mixed font, which CONVEYS THE CRAZY FEELING of NYC." —*Kelly purkey*

**NYC** *by Kelly Purkey*

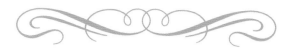

HOW cool ! Kelly's title treatment is über-creative, with her innovative combination of a star stamp, letter stickers and paint. Read on for an easy how-to.

① Stamp the star stamp repeatedly in black ink on your cardstock to form a pattern.

② Adhere a letter sticker to the stamped pattern. Cover it with white paint.

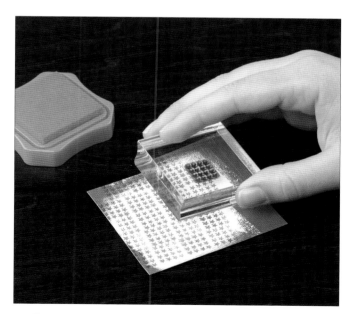

③ Stamp the star pattern again using orange ink, covering the top of the dried paint.

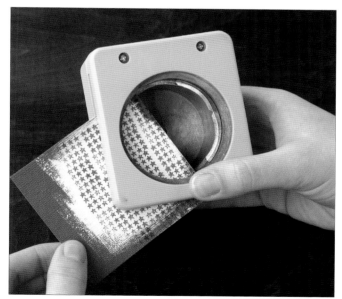

④ Punch out the stamped cardstock with a circle punch then carefully remove the letter sticker.

i love that you love to explore our big backyard. {exploring with mo...}

**BIG BACKYARD** *by Jennifer McGuire*

HOW cool! Resist techniques are so much fun—and the look is always awesome!
Try Jennifer's rub-on resist technique for your next page title. Here's how:
① Apply white rub-on letters to white cardstock.
② Paint over them with acrylic paint.
③ Gently rub away excess paint with a paper towel.

# jennifer mcguire on type techniques with traditional products

WE SAT DOWN WITH JENNIFER MCGUIRE TO TALK
ABOUT HER RUB-ON RESIST TECHNIQUE.

**WHAT MAKES THIS A FUN TECHNIQUE?**

This technique is like magic. At one moment, you see nothing. But after applying paint, the letters appear. So fun!

**WHAT TYPES OF PAGES WOULD THIS LOOK GOOD ON?**

This technique works great on any page. I especially like it on kid pages—the messy painted look is perfect.

**WHAT TIPS FOR SUCCESS WOULD YOU RECOMMEND TO READERS?**

If you paint over the letters and wipe them clean but notice part of a letter didn't rub on completely, just fill it in with a white pen.

**WHAT TYPES OF LETTERING PRODUCTS DO YOU RECOMMEND FOR THIS TECHNIQUE?**

Any white rub-ons will work. But you can also use letter stickers as a mask for paint. Just remove them when the paint dries.

**ARE THERE OTHER WAYS TO GET THIS COOL LOOK?**

Several! Here are some other resist techniques to try:

① Stamp letters with Tsukineko's VersaMark ink on white cardstock. Heat emboss with clear embossing powder. Use paint in the same way to create a resist.

② Instead of covering rub-ons with paint, try rubbing pigment ink over them.

③ You can also use letter stickers as a mask for pigment ink. Just remove them after the ink dries.

# Home
## DECOR
## PROJECTS

*chapter 3.5*

I remember doing a photo shoot at Becky Higgins' house and seeing her walls covered with fun, creative home-decor items she'd made using scrapbooking supplies and lettering products. Her favorite quotes are prominently displayed for all to see. I love that she uses type and scrapbooking products in a beautiful way in her home.

You can do this, too! Create a home-decor project that utilizes type in a hip way. Try creating a wall hanging by mixing letters. Or use letterforms to spell out words along the frame of a photo. Or create an oversized letter embellished with words starting with that letter. Get started with the ideas on the following pages.

"I wanted the **LOOK AND FEEL** of this quote to be youthful and fun—something that could be hung in a child's room." —*brian tippetts*

**IMAGINATION** *by Brian Tippetts*

HOW cool! Mix and match type styles to highlight key words in titles, quotes and journaling blocks. Notice how Brian limited the number of typefaces he used to two in order to maintain unity and create a clean look.

"Trace the shapes of PREMADE WOODEN LETTERS onto patterned paper. Cut out and decoupage the paper to the letters, then sand the EDGES for a smooth finish." —mou saha ʒ

**HOME** *by Mou Saha*

HOW cool! Mou added her own personal touches to this project by stamping a meaningful quote. She finished her creation with some light dabs of acrylic paint, a hint of ink along the edges and a bit of pen work to make her letters pop.

"These letters are **TEXTURED AND COLORED** to bring out the lighter
colors in the photo—a nice contrast to the darker frame and background."
—amy martin

PROMISE *by Amy Martin*

HOW cool! This frame is simple to use—it has a raised photo mount that already
includes a sticky back, making lining up and attaching the photo a snap.

"I knew I wanted to hang this piece in my DAUGHTER'S ROOM, so I used classic fonts to create a timeless feel. I chose a clean sans-serif font for the portrait so it WOULDN'T DISTRACT from the technique. The words are actually the lyrics to a song ('Beautiful Little Girl' by Cheri Keaggy) that I sing while I rock her to sleep." —deena wuest

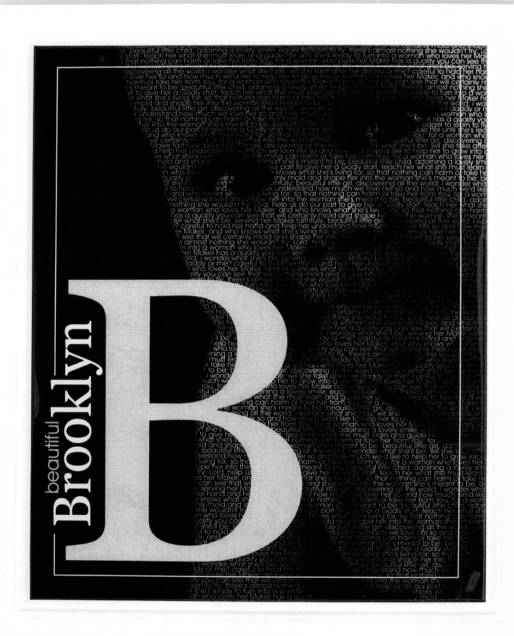

BEAUTIFUL BROOKLYN *by Deena Wuest*

HOW cool! It's easier than you think to create art from text using Photoshop Elements software. For this gorgeous effect, it's worth learning something new, don't you agree?

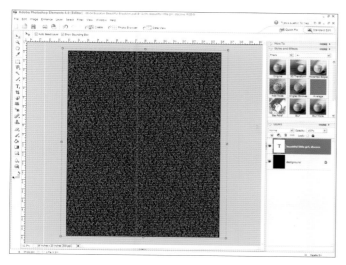

① Open a new 16" x 20" document in your photo-editing software. Change the background color to black. With the Horizontal Type tool, create a text box that is larger than the canvas. Type in your text and adjust the color to white. Highlight your text, then copy and paste it to fill your entire page.

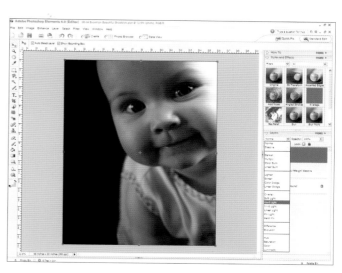

② Open your photo and enlarge it to fill the canvas. Make sure the photo is directly above your text in the Layers palette and change the photo-blending mode to Hard Light.

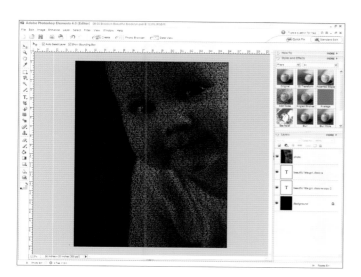

③ Adjust opacity and contrast until you achieve the look you want. (Here, Deena darkened her photo to create more shadow depth, and duplicated her white text layer to increase overall brightness.)

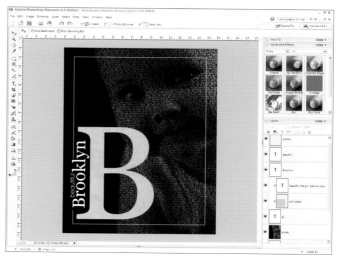

④ Add a monogram, title and border to complete your artwork. Upload it to your favorite online photo developer, then frame the print to hang in your home.

"To get just the **COLOR YOU WANT** for your fonts, use the Eyedropper tool in Photoshop Elements. For this layout, I changed the text color of each of **MY LINES**." —*elizabeth kartchner*

**LOOK HEAVENWARD** *by Elizabeth Kartchner*

HOW cool ! Choose a quote or saying that is special to your family. Use text boxes (or a separate layer) for each word to easily customize the placement of each piece of the quote. Notice how Elizabeth enlarged the quotation marks and used them to accent the quote.

"I used almost a **WHOLE ALPHABET** to cover the frame but still kept the look simple. A little pop of color in the tag and stars brightens the entire piece."

—*Kelly Purkey*

**E** *by Kelly Purkey*

HOW *cool*! Black stickers on a white frame provide a classic counterpart to the black-and-white photograph. Notice how Kelly chose a thin font that doesn't overwhelm the white frame.

"I wanted to design some **SPORTS CANVASES** for my nephew and loved the sporty look of the American Crafts stickers. Every letter of the alphabet is the **SAME HEIGHT**, creating such a cool look!" —*Laura Kurz*

**SPORTS CANVASES** *by Laura Kurz*

HOW cool! Though each of her canvases is a different color, Laura connected them to one another by using similar embellishments and sticking to a formula that includes a drawn pen line from the edge of each canvas to the beginning and end of the words.

"For this **MONOGRAM PROJECT**, I wanted a collage of different H's—
some bold and thick, and others thin; some serif and some sans serif."
—*maggie holmes*

**H** *by Maggie Holmes*

**HOW *cool*!** Maggie chose fonts she wanted to use and then added each letter to
her Photoshop document in layers. Leaving them each in their own layer made it
easy to manipulate and move each one around until she had the design arranged
just right. Once she had everything in place, she simply changed the colors until
the look suited her. She printed it out and then embellished with the butterflies
and brads.

"My sons are crazy about rockets right now, and a simple **ROCKET DRAWING** wouldn't suffice. Creating one out of chipboard letters was easy and fun!" —amanda probst

ROCKET IMAGINATION *by Amanda Probst*

HOW cool! Whether your gift recipient is into rockets, rainbows or running, you can use letters to create a shape that represents his or her interest. Here's how:

① Gather enough chipboard letters to create the shape. Don't be afraid to use a variety of chipboard sets.

② Paint all of the chipboard and a blank backing (the sheet of cardboard that comes with paper orders works well). For the letters, you'll need more than one coat of paint to hide the different patterns and colors you'll be starting with.

③ Adhere your letters to the backing in the shape desired. Use a craft knife or scissors to trim around the shape. Add embellishments.

④ Create the background using an appropriate patterned paper. If desired, add additional materials to the background. Here, Amanda hand-cut a curve of cardstock and applied tiny letter stickers for the quote.

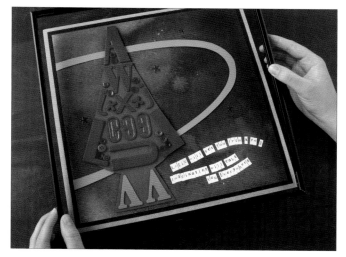

⑤ Adhere your shape to the background paper, then frame your creation.

# Technique FUN

If it's taking hours to find just the right typeface to mix with another, consider a different way to mix up your type. A start? Try combining different type mediums: a font with letter stickers or maybe rub-ons with chipboard letters. The addition of a different texture or color may be just what you're looking for.

Another solution? Try different text effects to customize your type selections. Don't be afraid to mix it up! On the following pages, get more ideas for customizing your titles and journaling. Take a look!

## MIX & MATCH TYPE TECHNIQUES

Don't be afraid to use more than one type medium on a single layout—you'll love the textural richness and visual interest it brings to your page. We asked Maggie and Mou to mix and match type mediums—take a look at what they came up with!

**HOW cool!** Maggie used four type mediums on this layout: chipboard, stamps, rub-ons and her own handwriting. Notice how the chipboard, stamps and rub-on all feature a similar serif.

**AS YOU GROW** *by Maggie Holmes*

"Since SPELLING OUT 'You' in the same font would have overwhelmed the card, I just used a red individual letter sticker INSTEAD." —*mou saha*

**HOW cool!** Because she used an outline font stamp, Mou could choose any paper that fit the theme of her card. The tropical colors of the patterned papers didn't require additional embellishments and helped Mou keep the design clean and simple. Looking for a good way to repurpose paper scraps? Stamp and cut out letters for cards or page titles.

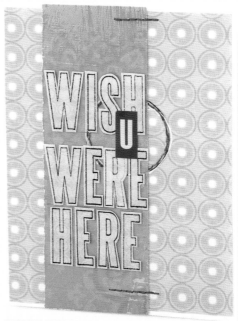

**"WISH U WERE HERE" CARD** *by Mou Saha*

## 1 PAGE, 3 TEXT EFFECTS

Today's technology allows you to manipulate your text in remarkable and creative ways. More than just words on a page, your text is an important design element, and by utilizing text effects you can elevate your projects from adequate to amazing. Deena Wuest created three versions of the same layout to show just how powerful and distinct text effects can be.

Look mom! I've got the

static

"eclecktity"

age five

**STATIC "ECLECKTITY"** *by Deena Wuest*

## ELECTRIC ^

① Using the Horizontal Type tool, type in your title.

② Right-click on your text in the Layers palette and select Simplify Layer.

③ Duplicate this layer and hide it from view in the Layers palette.

④ Rotate the original text image 90 degrees and apply the Wind filter by selecting Filter > Stylize > Wind, with Direction from the Right highlighted. Repeat this filter by pressing Ctrl+F.

⑤ Apply the Wind filter two more times using the Direction from the Left option.

⑥ Rotate your image back to its original position and repeat the above process, applying only one Wind filter in each direction.

⑦ To create the wavy effect, apply the Ripple filter by selecting Filter > Distort > Ripple.

⑧ Unhide the second text image and position it above the edited layer.

⑨ Adjust color and opacity as desired.

Though it takes longer to achieve, this effect goes beyond adorning a title and becomes a unique page element that not only embellishes the page, but also reinforces the theme of the layout. (Psst! This one is Deena's favorite!)

<< PLASTIC WRAP

① Using the Horizontal Type tool, type in your title.

② Right-click on your text in the Layers palette and select Simplify Layer.

③ In the Styles and Effects palette, select Filters.

④ Click and drag Plastic Wrap directly onto your text.

⑤ Adjust the Strength, Detail and Smoothness until you achieve the look you want.

The solid yellow color of this title really makes a bold statement.

...............................................

"If you want to make a STRONG STATEMENT with your title, you can never go wrong with IMPACT. It's bold, striking and a perfect FONT for this page about my daughter. For contrast, I paired it with a DELICATE but clean font, Geosans Light."

—deena wuest

...............................................

HOW cool! Deena tried out three different title effects. You can achieve them yourself using Photoshop Elements. Which do you feel is most effective?

<< OUTLINE

① Using the Horizontal Type Mask tool, type in your title.

② Select the Rectangular Marquee tool.

③ Go to Edit and select Stroke. Set the pixel width and color then click OK.

This title lends a graphic but airy feel to the layout.

## FONT MAKEOVER

Admit it. You love fonts. That's why you're reading this book! Chances are, your font library is fairly extensive, and you frequently find yourself mulling over font choices when you're creating. Finding just the right font can be fun or frustrating, but when choosing a font style for a journaling block, it's imperative that your words are readable. So when you're tempted to use a stylized typeset in a block of journaling, step away! Take it from Kelly Purkey, who's been there.

**EAT** *by Kelly Purkey*

## BEFORE ∧

Kelly wanted to highlight certain words and phrases in her journaling block, and she knew that varying the type would do the trick. In her first version, the script font she selected has several problems: it's tough to read, its size doesn't seem to match her main font, and it's too fancy for a layout about a fun, casual eating experience.

"I added the TEXT BLOCKS in the grouping of photos at the last minute to indicate some of the menu selections. The patterned-paper squares were ORIGINALLY BLANK, but they needed something on them to stand up to the busy, bold photos." —*Kelly Purkey*

**AFTER**

In the second rendering, Kelly found a font that works much better with her page. Not only is it much more readable, but it also mimics the curves of the restaurant's logo and fits in nicely with the mood of her layout.

# Supplies

A NOTE ABOUT FONT SOURCES: You'll notice that many supply lists include only the font name. These fonts are available from multiple online vendors. You can use your favorite online search engine to find these fonts for purchase or free download.

.............................................

"When the type is POORLY CHOSEN, what the words say linguistically and what the LETTERS IMPLY VISUALLY are disharmonious, dishonest, out of tune."
—robert bringhurst

23 • **On Target** *by Amanda Probst.* **Supplies** *Cardstock:* Prism Papers; *Chipboard letters:* Junkitz; *Paint:* Making Memories; *Pen:* Precision Pen, American Crafts; *Font:* Rockwell.

24 • **Ours** *by Laura Kurz.* **Supplies** *Cardstock:* Bazzill Basics Paper; *Letter stamp:* FontWerks; *Ink:* Close To My Heart; *Font:* American Typewriter.

25 • **Further Proof** *by Deena Wuest.* **Supplies** *Software:* Adobe Photoshop Elements 4.0; *Digital paper:* Peas-n-Carrots Paper Pack by Katie Pertiet, www.designerdigitals.com; *Digital page template (revised):* Tortuga Template No. 33 by Kellie Mize, www.designerdigitals.com; *Fonts:* Impact and Rockwell.

26 • **At 3** *by Mou Saha.* **Supplies** *Cardstock:* Frances Meyer; *Letter stickers:* BasicGrey, Chatterbox, Doodlebug Design and SEI; *Cardstock stickers:* 7gypsies; *Embroidery floss:* DMC; *Pen:* American Crafts; *Font:* Tigger.

27 • **Grow Like a Weed** *by Amy Martin.* **Supplies** *Software:* Paint Shop Pro XI, Corel; *Digital paper, word art and ribbons:* Bottoms Up! Kit by Amy Hutchinson, www.amyhutchinsondesigns.com; *Digital Bingo pieces:* Spanish Garden by Amy Hutchinson, www.weare-storytellers.net; *Digital heart:* Michelle Godin, www.the-lilypad.com; *Digital staples:* Backward Staples, Jenn Patrick; *Font:* Times New Roman.

28 • **Chloe** *by Kelly Purkey.* **Supplies** *Software:* Adobe Photoshop Elements 7.0; *Cardstock:* Core'dinations and Prism Papers; *Patterned paper:* American Crafts (blue polka dot), Heidi Grace Designs (purple, pink, blue paisley), KI Memories (green), Making Memories (scallop edge) and Scenic Route (cream); *Tag and brads:* Making Memories; *Rub-ons:* We R Memory Keepers; *Decorative-edge scissors:* Fiskars; *Photo corners:* American Crafts; *Fonts:* Establo and ShagExpert, House Industries; *Other:* Embroidery floss.

31 • **Once Upon a Time** *by Brian Tippetts.* **Supplies** *Cardstock:* Prism Papers; *Photo corners:* Canson; *Fonts:* Gigi, Letraset and Olduvai, Umbrella Type for www.veer.com.

32 • **Amy** *by Brian Tippetts.* **Supplies** *Patterned paper:* Tinkering Ink (gray), Ultimate Flower Kit, CK Media (flower print) and Love, Elsie by KI Memories (green); *Chipboard:* Ultimate Flower Kit, CK Media (flower) and Cosmo Cricket (letters); *Paint:* Delta Creative; *Pen:* Galaxy Marker, American Crafts; *Font:* Trixie, www.fontfont.com.

33 • **My Best Skyler Wuest** *by Deena Wuest.* **Supplies** *Software:* Adobe Photoshop Elements 4.0; *Digital paper:* Purely Happy Paper Pack by Katie Pertiet, www.designerdigitals.com; *Digital border:* Graphic Pop Edgers Brushes-n-Stamps by Katie Pertiet, www.designerdigitals.com; *Fonts:* Avant Garde and Establo.

34 • **No** *by Elizabeth Kartchner.* **Supplies** *Software:* Adobe Photoshop Elements 6.0; *Cardstock:* Bazzill Basics Paper; *Patterned paper:* Sassafras Lass; *Chipboard hearts:* Heidi Swapp for Advantus; *Clear tape:* Prima; *Vinyl letters:* American Crafts; *Fabric tape:* Martha Stewart Crafts; *Flowers:* Making Memories; *Fonts:* 2Peas Dressy Dots, www.twopeasinabucket.com; Mia's Scribblings and Little Days; *Other:* Heart buttons and thread.

35 • **Rolling** *by Maggie Holmes.* **Supplies** *Cardstock:* Prism Papers; *Patterned paper:* Creative Imaginations and Sassafras Lass; *Chipboard shapes, letter stickers, die cut and brads:* Making Memories; *Stamp:* FontWerks; *Ink:* ColorBox, Clearsnap; *Flowers:* Making Memories and Prima; *Tab:* Creative Imaginations; *Corner punch:* Fiskars; *Pen:* Zig Writer, EK Success; *Font:* Cafeina Dig.

36 • **You Can't Always Get What You Want** *by Ali Edwards.* **Supplies** *Cardstock:* Bazzill Basics Paper; *Date stamp:* OfficeMax; *Ink:* ColorBox, Clearsnap; *Circle cutter:* Creative Memories; *Foam squares:* Scrapbook Adhesives by 3L; *Pen:* American Crafts; *Dingbat:* Bookshelf Symbol 7, Microsoft; *Font:* Century Gothic.

"Good TYPOGRAPHY HELPS PEOPLE read your copy, while bad typography prevents them from doing so." —*David Ogilvy*

39 • **Nature Child** *by Amy Martin.* **Supplies** *Software:* Paint Shop Pro XI, Corel; *Digital paper:* About Us Paper by Natalie Braxton, www.the-lilypad.com; Legible Set No. 1 by Meredith Fenwick, www.scrapbookgraphics.com; *Digital labels:* Quote Coasters and Woven T-Shirt Labels, www.jenwilsondesigns.com; *Digital buttons:* Addon Elements—Dude by Amy Hutchinson, www.amy-hutchinsondesigns.com; *Digital circle:* Glitter Circles by Lori Barnhurst, www.littledreamerdesigns.com; *Digital bird:* Quirky Birds No. 1 by Jackie Eckles, www.littledreamerdesigns.com; *Digital swirls:* Whimsical Swirls by Jenna Desai, www.the-lilypad.com; *Digital word stickers:* Family Word Stickers by Amy Wolff, www.the-lilypad.com; *Fonts:* CK Dirty (title, version 1), www.creatingkeepsakes.com; Hand Stamped Alpha (title, version 2), www.littledreamerdesigns.com; 1942 Report.

40 • **A Helping Hand** *by Amanda Probst.* **Supplies** *Cardstock:* Prism Papers; *Fonts:* CK Taliatype (journaling, version 1) and CK Tatty (title, version 2), www.creatingkeepsakes.com; Karabine (title, version 1), Impact (title, version 3), Typist (journaling, version 2) and Rockwell (journaling, version 3).

42 • **"Happy Birthday" Card** *by Deena Wuest.* **Supplies** *Software:* Adobe Photoshop Elements 4.0; *Digital page template (revised):* Tortuga Template by Kellie Mize; *Digital flower:* Whimsical II Custom Shapes by Anna Aspnes, www.designerdigitals.com; *Font:* Interstate-Light.

43 • **One Wish** *by Kelly Purkey.* **Supplies** *Software:* Adobe Photoshop Elements 7.0; *Cardstock:* Core'dinations; *Patterned paper:* Heidi Grace Designs (green circle) and Making Memories (multicolor circle); *Paper file:* BasicGrey; *Decorative-edge scissors, circle punch and corner rounder:* Fiskars; *Tag:* Making Memories; *Buttons:* American Crafts and Autumn Leaves; *Brads:* American Crafts; *Font:* Pretty Baby.

47 • **"You Rock!" Card** *by Amanda Probst.* **Supplies** *Cardstock:* Prism Papers; *Clear gloss:* Glossy Accents, Ranger Industries; *Pens:* Gelly Roll, Sakura; *Fonts:* Kravitz; TXT Soda Shoppe and DB Party Sketch, www.scrapnfonts.com.

48 • **"Happy Birthday" Card** *by Maggie Holmes.* **Supplies** *Cardstock:* Prism Papers; *Patterned paper:* Sassafras Lass; *Brads:* Making Memories; *Fonts:* Cairo and Seeing Stars.

49 • **Birthdays** *by Deena Wuest.* **Supplies** *Software:* Adobe Photoshop Elements 4.0; *Digital paper:* Happy as a Lark Paper Pack by Paislee Press, www.oscraps.com; *Digital page template (revised):* Tortuga Template No. 37 by Kellie Mize, www.designerdigitals.com; *Fonts:* JLR Birthday Banner and Gregor Miller's Friends Font.

"Typography has ONE PLAIN DUTY before it and that is to convey information in writing."

—emil ruder

"Type well used is INVISIBLE AS TYPE, just as the perfect talking voice is the unnoticed VEHICLE for the transmission of words, ideas."
— beatrice warde

## CHAPTER 2.5

99 • **Every Flower** by Amy Martin. **Supplies** Software: Paint Shop Pro XI, Corel; Digital paper: Charmes d'antan, www.oscraps.com; Digital feather, felt and wooden frames: Not Very Serious by Jofia Devoe, www.shabbypickledesigns.com; Digital brushes: Floral Spray Wildflowers by Michelle Coleman, www.littledreamerdesigns.com; Digital brads: The Ol' Switcheroo Backwards Brads by Karah Fredricks, www.thedigichick.com; Digital word labels: Wordy Chips, www.jenwilsondesigns.com; Fonts: SimSun, Last Words, LainyDay Script and LDJ Silly Sister.

## CHAPTER 3.1

103 • **Blue Alphabet** by Brian Tippetts. **Supplies** Software: Adobe Illustrator CS3; Font: Perla-Regular, www.veer.com.

103 • **"Oh, Boy!" Card** by Laura Kurz. **Supplies** Cardstock and letter stickers: American Crafts.

104 • **"Name That Font" Game** by Erin Bayless. **Supplies** Cardstock: Bazzill Basics Paper; Corner rounder: Marvy Uchida; Fonts: Affair, www.veer.com; Benton, Font Bureau; Brothers Regular, Emigre Fonts; Engravers Old English, Monotype Imaging; Eurostile Normal and Edwardian Script, Linotype; Gotham, Hoefler & Frere-Jones; AG Book Rounded Outline, Aachen, Adobe Garamond, Bodoni Classic Chancery, Bodoni, Carnivale, Clarendon Bold, Commercial Script, Craw Modern Italic, Didot Light, Din Black, Dorchester Script, Duc de Berry, Eclat, Fling, Flemish Script, French Script and Futura Black.

105 • **PSA** by Amanda Probst. **Supplies** Cardstock: Prism Papers; Chipboard people: Maya Road; Clear gloss: Glossy Accents, Ranger Industries; Corner rounder: EK Success; Fonts: Alba, Century Gothic, Pegsanna and Sketch Rockwell.

106 • **"Butterfly" Card** by Janice Barfuss. **Supplies** Cards and envelopes: Paper Accents, Petersen-Arne; Font: Affair, www.veer.com.

107 • **Watch It Grow** by Mou Saha. **Supplies** Cardstock: Die Cuts With a View; Patterned paper: BasicGrey; Letter stickers: American Crafts, Doodlebug Design, Making Memories and SEI; Square punch: Marvy Uchida; Ink: Tsukineko.

108 • **"Save Our Planet" T-Shirt** by Natalie Reich. **Supplies** T-shirt: REI; Iron-on: Inkjet T-shirt Transfers, Avery; Fonts: Animals by Alan Carr; Clarendon; Recycle It by Barmee; Type Embellishments Two, Letraset.

108 • **"Wish You Were Here" Card** by Elizabeth Kartchner. **Supplies** Software: Adobe Photoshop Elements 6.0; Cardstock: Epson; Patterned paper: October Afternoon and Sassafras Lass; Foam shapes, brads and ribbon: American Crafts; Stamps: Green Grass Stamps; Ink: StazOn, Tsukineko; Button: Making Memories; Font: Sue Ellen Francisco.

109 • **You Are Loved** by Laura Kurz. **Supplies** Cardstock: American Crafts and Bazzill Basics Paper; Letter stickers: American Crafts; Butterfly punch: Martha Stewart Crafts; Font: American Typewriter.

110 • **"Your Words" Cards** by Nicole LaRue. **Supplies** Paper and envelope: xpedx; Type: Nicole's own design.

111 • **Daily Routine** by Elizabeth Kartchner. **Supplies** Software: Adobe Photoshop Elements 6.0; Cardstock: Epson; Patterned paper: American Crafts, Heidi Swapp for Advantus, KI Memories, October Afternoon and Sassafras Lass; Sticker: American Crafts; Brad: Creative Imaginations; Word sticker: Daisy D's Paper Co.; Clock and heart accents: Heidi Swapp for Advantus; Rhinestones: Karen Foster Design and Glitz Design; Flower charm: KI Memories; Fonts: CK Ali's Writing, www.creatingkeepsakes.com; Fabianestem, Laundromat 1967 and Scream.

## CHAPTER 3.2

113 • **My Little Ellie** by Brian Tippetts. **Supplies** Software: Adobe Illustrator; Flowers: Brian's own designs; Font: Peach Fuzz, www.fontbros.com.

114 • **Submit. Pray. Celebrate. Repeat.** by Deena Wuest. **Supplies** Software: Adobe Photoshop Elements 4.0; Font: Garamond Pro.

115 • **Beautiful Colors** by Kelly Purkey. **Supplies** Software: Adobe Photoshop Elements 7.0; Patterned paper: BasicGrey (stripe), Heidi Grace Designs (green, brown polka dot) and Scenic Route (yellow dot); Rub-ons: American Crafts and BasicGrey; Brads: American Crafts; Leaf punch: Fiskars; Digital brushes: Rhonna Swirls, www.twopeasinabucket.com; Font: Rosewood.

116 • **Sushi Love** by Elizabeth Kartchner. **Supplies** Software: Adobe Photoshop Elements 6.0; Patterned paper: American Crafts (yellow and brown) and Prima (red, orange and blue); Clear tape: Prima; Buttons: KI Memories and Making Memories; Pins: Heidi Grace Designs; Brads: American Crafts and Doodlebug Design; Fonts: Boris Black Bloxx; 2Peas Cross Eyed, www.two-peasinabucket.com.

118 • **I Love You** by Jessica Sprague. **Supplies** Cardstock: Bazzill Basics Paper; Patterned paper: Cosmo Cricket and K&Company; Flowers: Prima; Digital photo flourish: Hipster Plumes Brush Set by Anna Aspnes, www.designerdigitals.com; Chipboard letters: Chatterbox; Rhinestone brads: SEI; Font: Century Gothic; Other: Chipboard heart.

"Typography is not self expression with PREDETERMINED AESTHETICS; it is conditioned by the message it visualizes."
—herbert bayer

## CHAPTER 3.3

121 • **Eyes** by Amy Martin. **Supplies** Software: Paint Shop Pro XI, Corel; Digital paper: Melon Madness by Amy Hutchinson, www.amyhutchinsondesigns.com; Digital frames: Circle Frames by Amy Wolff, www.the-lilypad.com; Digital flowers: Punky Petals by Kate Hadfield, www.the-lilypad.com; Digital notebook paper: Amy Martin, www.the-lilypad.com; Digital journaling strips: Fee Jardin, www.sweetshoppedesigns.com; Digital staples: Plum Yum Mega Element Pack by Lisa Whitney, www.scrapartist.com; Digital stitched frame: Quirky Stitches by Jackie Eckles, www.littledreamerdesigns.com; Embroidery floss: DMC; Fonts: Arial; CK Little Buggy, www.creatingkeepsakes.com.

122 • **Dinosaurs Then & Now** by Mou Saha. **Supplies** Software: Adobe Photoshop Elements 5.0; Cardstock: Frances Meyer; Acetate letters: Heidi Swapp for Advantus; Ink: Adirondack Alcohol Ink, Ranger Industries; Pens: American Crafts (black) and Marvy Uchida (red); Fonts: American Typewriter and Dirty Ego.

123 • **365 Days** by Deena Wuest. **Supplies** Software: Adobe Photoshop Elements 4.0; Cardstock: WorldWin; Patterned paper, ribbon and resin pebble: Masterpiece Studios; Chipboard letters: Rusty Pickle; Digital paper: Purely Happy Paper Pack by Katie Pertiet, www.designerdigitals.com; Fonts: CK Ali's Writing and LB Hodge Podge, www.creatingkeepsakes.com; Avant Garde, Eurostile, Gill Sans, Georgia and Impact.

124 • **Paradise** by Jessica Sprague. **Supplies** Cardstock: Bazzill Basics Paper; Patterned paper: Creative Imaginations; Digital paper (behind journaling): La Paperie No. 1 by Jen Wilson, www.jenwilsondesigns.com; Chipboard swirl: Fancy Pants Designs; Fonts: Century Gothic and You Are Loved; Other: Buttons.

126 • **Ancora Imparo** by Amanda Probst. **Supplies** *Cardstock:* Prism Papers; *Chipboard letters:* Li'l Davis Designs; *Mini letter stickers:* Making Memories; *Acetate flourish:* My Mind's Eye; *Photo corners:* Scrapbook Adhesives by 3L; *Fonts:* CK Chemistry, www.creatingkeepsakes.com; TXT Stonewashed, www.scrapnfonts.com.

127 • **Love Family** by Laura Kurz. **Supplies** *Cardstock and pen:* American Crafts; *Letter stickers:* Doodlebug Design; *Brads:* American Crafts; *Font:* Garamond.

128 • **Jack O Lanterns** by Mou Saha. **Supplies** *Software:* Adobe Photoshop Elements 5.0; *Cardstock:* Frances Meyer; *Letter stickers:* American Crafts and Making Memories; *Cardstock tab:* Déjà Views, The C-Thru Ruler Co.; *Brad:* Making Memories; *Pens:* Newell Rubbermaid (white) and Sakura (orange); *Font:* Nerve Tonic.

## CHAPTER 3.4

131 • **Pretty Girl** by Maggie Holmes. **Supplies** *Cardstock:* Prism Papers; *Patterned paper:* Prima and Sassafras Lass; *Ribbon:* Making Memories; *Rub-ons:* Cosmo Cricket; *Stamped tag, notecard, fabric yo-yo's and buttons:* The Scarlet Lime; *Letter die cuts:* Making Memories; *Pen:* Zig Writer, EK Success.

131 • **Up You Go** by Amy Martin. **Supplies** *Software:* Paint Shop Pro XI, Corel; *Digital paper:* About Us Paper by Natalie Braxton, www.the-lilypad.com; Legible Set No. 1 by Meredith Fenwick, www.scrapbookgraphics.com; *Digital labels:* Quote Coasters and Woven T-Shirt Labels by Jen Wilson, www.jenwilsondesigns.com; *Digital buttons:* Addon Elements—Dude by Amy Hutchinson, www.amyhutchinsondesigns.com; *Digital circles:* Glitter Circles by Lori Barnhurst, www.littledreamerdesigns.com; *Digital bird:* Quirky Birds by Jackie Eckles, www.littledreamerdesigns.com; *Digital swirls:* Whimsical Swirls by Jenna Desai, www.the-lilypad.com; *Digital word stickers:* Family Word Stickers by Amy Wolff, www.the-lilypad.com; *Fonts:* Hand Stamped Alphas, www.littledreamerdesigns.com; 1942 Report.

132 • **NYC** by Kelly Purkey. **Supplies** *Cardstock:* Core'dinations; *Patterned paper:* Doodlebug Design (red), Heidi Grace Designs (blue dot) and KI Memories (orange and stripe); *Stickers:* American Crafts and Creative Imaginations; *Brads:* American Crafts; *Star punch, circle template and corner rounder:* Fiskars; *Stamp:* FontWerks; *Ink:* StazOn, Tsukineko; *Paint:* Making Memories; *Font:* SP Purkalator, www.scrapsupply.com.

134 • **Big Backyard** by Jennifer McGuire. **Supplies** *Cardstock:* Bazzill Basics Paper; *Rub-ons:* American Crafts; *Buttons:* Autumn Leaves; *Paint:* Adirondack Acrylic Paint Dabbers, Ranger Industries; *Other:* String.

## CHAPTER 3.5

137 • **Imagination** by Brian Tippetts. **Supplies** *Software:* Adobe Photoshop CS3; *Patterned paper:* Tinkering Ink; *Fonts:* Emmascript Standard, MVB; New Century Schoolbook Roman, Adobe Systems.

138 • **Home** by Mou Saha. **Supplies** *Patterned paper:* Autumn Leaves (plaid), Frances Meyer (cream paisley) and Making Memories (kraft); *Letter stamps:* K&Company; *Letter stickers:* Making Memories; *Cardstock stickers:* 7gypsies; *Ink and paint:* Ranger Industries; *Wooden letter set:* Adornit - Carolee's Creations; *Pen:* Newell Rubbermaid; *Other:* Craft knife and sandpaper.

139 • **Promise** by Amy Martin. **Supplies** *Flowers, letters, jewels and brads:* Prima; *Frame:* Target.

140 • **Beautiful Brooklyn** by Deena Wuest. **Supplies** *Software:* Adobe Photoshop Elements 4.0; *Digital paper:* Nursery Paper Pack by Katie Pertiet, www.designerdigitals.com; *Fonts:* Avant Garde and Garamond Pro.

142 • **Look Heavenward** by Elizabeth Kartchner. **Supplies** *Software:* Adobe Photoshop Elements 6.0; *Cardstock:* Bazzill Basics Paper; *Clips:* Making Memories; *Font:* American Typewriter.

143 • **E** by Kelly Purkey. Photo by Susan Weinroth. **Supplies** *Cardstock:* Core'dinations; *Patterned paper:* Heidi Grace Designs; *Stickers and brad:* American Crafts; *Star and circle punches:* Fiskars.

144 • **Sports Canvases** by Laura Kurz. **Supplies** *Letter stickers and pen:* American Crafts; *Paint and epoxy shapes:* Making Memories.

145 • **H** by Maggie Holmes. **Supplies** *Glitter adhesive paper and brads:* Making Memories; *Butterfly punch:* Martha Stewart Crafts; *Acrylic frame:* Target; *Fonts:* Bookman Old Style, Cairo, Fabianestem, FranKlein Bold, Haettenschweiler, Impact and Modern No. 20.

146 • **Imagination** by Amanda Probst. **Supplies** *Cardstock:* Prism Papers; *Patterned paper:* Wordsworth; *Letters:* Li'l Davis Designs, Scenic Route and Target; *Paint and mini letter stickers:* Making Memories; *Clear gloss:* Glossy Accents, Ranger Industries; *Buttons:* foof-a-La, Autumn Leaves; *Other:* Frame.

> "Typographical design should perform OPTICALLY what the SPEAKER CREATES through voice and gesture of his thoughts."
> —el lizzitsky?

## CHAPTER 3.6

149 • **As You Grow** by Maggie Holmes. **Supplies** *Cardstock:* Prism Papers; *Patterned paper:* GCD Studios and We R Memory Keepers; *Chipboard stars:* Bazzill Basics Paper and Creative Imaginations; *Clear stamps:* FontWerks; *Rub-ons and tickets:* Jenni Bowlin Studio; *Ink:* StazOn, Tsukineko; *Chipboard letters, ribbon and brads:* Making Memories; *Pen:* American Crafts.

149 • **"Wish U Were Here" Card** by Mou Saha. **Supplies** *Patterned paper:* Frances Meyer (gray and blue) and Junkitz (orange); *Letter stamps:* FontWerks; *Letter stickers:* Heidi Swapp for Advantus; *Ink:* Tsukineko; *Card:* Halcraft USA; *Embroidery floss:* DMC.

150 • **Static Eclecktity** by Deena Wuest. **Supplies** *Software:* Adobe Photoshop Elements 4.0; *Digital paper:* Reservoir Paper Pack by Katie Pertiet, www.designerdigitals.com; *Digital paper edges:* Simple Torn Edges No. 6 by Anna Aspnes, www.designerdigitals.com; *Digital mask:* Basic Masking Gradients by Anna Aspnes, www.designerdigitals.com; *Fonts:* Geo Sans Light and Impact.

152 • **Eat** by Kelly Purkey. **Supplies** *Software:* Adobe Photoshop Elements 7.0; *Cardstock:* Core'dinations and Prism Papers; *Patterned paper:* Heidi Grace Designs (yellow), K&Company (blue dot and green dot) and SEI (tea flower); *Stickers, brad, rub-ons and button:* American Crafts; *Circle punch:* Fiskars; *Stamp:* Hero Arts; *Fonts:* American Typewriter, English 111 and Futura.

> "Letters are THINGS, not pictures of things."
> —eric gill

# cool things

*by brian tippetts*

## 5 things to typographically inspire you today

### 1. GREAT TOOL

Need a little help determining the exact size of your text before you print it for a title or journaling block? Open the type ruler I've designed for you on this book's bonus CD. Print the ruler on a transparency and position it over a journaling block to choose the perfect text size and fit.

### 2. OUTSIDE INSPIRATION

Looking for some cool letters to hang in your space? Check out your local Anthropologie store. They've got decorative letters made from wood, metal and even fabric.

### 3. FREE FONTS

Do you love free fonts? Bookmark *www.dafont.com*. Boasting over 8,000 fonts, it's sure to have a few (or a lot) that you want/need/must download now! Check out the custom preview feature that lets you test drive your font before you download it.

### 4. HELPFUL WEBSITE

Psst. Here's a little designer tip. If you're looking for the coolest fonts of the moment, go to *www.veer.com*. It's a website for professional designers and includes awesome typefaces, interesting photography and great, free desktop wallpaper. Be sure to check out the cool type merchandise, like my Kern jacket (see back cover).

### 5. TYPE TRIVIA

Need a new bit of trivia to wow your scrapbooking pals? Tell them about the interrobang. This seldom used punctuation mark is a combination of the question mark (interrogative point) and the exclamation point (called the "bang" in printer's slang). Its intended use is for expressions requiring both marks, in questions such as "You did what?!" It was introduced by Martin K. Speckter in 1962. Look for this symbol in open type fonts like Palatino Linotype, Calibri and Arial Unicode MS.